100 PROOFS THAT
JESUS IS GOD

100 PROOFS THAT
JESUS IS GOD

Curt D. Daniel

Reformation Heritage Books
Grand Rapids, Michigan

Reformation Heritage Books
3070 29th St. SE
Grand Rapids, MI 49512
616-977-0889
orders@heritagebooks.org
www.heritagebooks.org

Printed in the United States of America
24 25 26 27 28/10 9 8 7 6 5 4 3 2

Library of Congress Cataloging-in-Publication Data

Names: Daniel, Curt, author.
Title: 100 proofs that Jesus is God / Curt D. Daniel.
Other titles: One hundred proofs that Jesus is God
Description: Grand Rapids, Michigan : Reformation Heritage Books, [2023]
Identifiers: LCCN 2023026796 (print) | LCCN 2023026797 (ebook) |
    ISBN 9798886860443 (paperback) | ISBN 9798886860450 (epub)
Subjects: LCSH: God—Biblical teaching. | Jesus Christ—Person and offices. |
    Bible—Evidences, authority, etc.
Classification: LCC BS544 .D36 2023 (print) | LCC BS544 (ebook) |
    DDC 231—dc23/eng/20230703
LC record available at https://lccn.loc.gov/2023026796
LC ebook record available at https://lccn.loc.gov/2023026797

Contents

Foreword

John Owen said, "One of the greatest privileges and advancements of believers, both in this world and unto eternity, consists in their beholding the glory of Christ."[1] And we see His glory only when we recognize that He is no mere man, but the God-man, God the Son incarnate. Therefore, it is a great help to believers to see how the Bible reveals the deity of Christ in many ways, and by God's grace such knowledge can be a powerful persuasive for an unbeliever to become a believer.

This book is especially helpful for four reasons. First, it is *concise*. Each proof for the deity of Christ is presented briefly so that the reader can quickly read it, perhaps in his daily devotions. There are no long discussions of theology here, just golden nuggets of sound doctrine. Second, it is *manifold*. No less than a hundred proofs are offered, what the author calls an "avalanche of evidence." Unbelievers might dodge a few of these proofs, but the sheer weight of the Bible's testimony that Christ is God is difficult for an honest reader to avoid. Third, it is *biblical*. The author grounds each proof in the plain words of the Holy Scriptures. This allows the reader to see that the Christian faith is not invented by some church council but is revealed by God in His Word. Fourth, it is *rich*. By drawing from many different passages and themes of Scripture, the book encourages us to meditate on everything Christ does as a display of His deity, from His teaching to His second coming.

---

1. John Owen, *Meditations and Discourses on the Glory of Christ*, in *The Works of John Owen*, ed. William H. Goold (New York: Robert Carter & Brothers, 1850), 1:286.

Books such as this are greatly needed today. Much that passes for Christianity is doctrinally anemic, lacking a vigorous embrace of the biblical gospel. The "Jesus" of popular piety is often little more than an empathetic friend, not the Lord of glory. And false teachers are busy drawing disciples after themselves instead of preaching the only begotten Son in His divine majesty and eternal love. May God use this short book of my good and faithful friend, Dr. Curt Daniel, for the glory of His triune name, and to strengthen His church "till we all come in the unity of the faith, and of the knowledge of the Son of God" (Eph. 4:13).

—Joel R. Beeke

Introduction

The purpose of this little book is to prove from the Bible that Jesus Christ is God. It is based on the Bible alone, not other sources. Most creeds, churches, and theologians have affirmed the deity of Christ. But if the Bible says otherwise, they are wrong. If, however, the Bible does indeed teach that Jesus is God, then any person or church denying this is wrong.

I invite you to be like the noble Bereans who "searched the Scriptures daily" to see if these things were so (Acts 17:11). God urges us to "test all things; hold fast what is good" (1 Thess. 5:21). You are encouraged to look up the Bible verses and see for yourself what God Himself says. You may even wish to skip the explanations and just consult the Bible itself. You may also want to test the writings of those who deny that Christ is God, and remember what God says in Isaiah 8:20: "To the law and to the testimony! If they do not speak according to this word, it is because there is no light in them."

This book is written for three kinds of readers. First, it is for those who already believe Jesus is God. These pages will help them see the richness of this wonderful truth in ways they may not have imagined. Second, it is for those who deny that Jesus is God. Perhaps a friend has given you this book. Please accept it in the kind spirit in which it is meant. Third, it is for those who admit they do not know. This little guide will help show you what the Bible itself says.

The proofs have been organized under one hundred brief statements. Some contain many Bible verses; others, only one or two. Some proofs are explicit; others, implicit. Many of them overlap. Undoubtedly there are still many more.

My approach is to give as many verses and proofs as possible. I employ what lawyers might call the "avalanche of evidence" approach. Someone might be able to dodge a few rocks in an avalanche—but not all. Someone might explain away some of these proofs—but not all. All it takes is one. The preponderance of proof is clearly on the side of the deity of Christ.

After I finished writing this book, I came across a very rare little book titled *Several Hundred Texts of Holy Scripture, Plainly Proving That Our Lord Jesus Christ Is the Most High God: Collected, Compared, and Disposed in a Proper Method* by an anonymous "Presbyter of the Church of England." I also discovered a rare pamphlet titled *More Than One Hundred Scriptural and Incontrovertible Arguments for Believing in the Deity of Our Lord and Saviour Jesus Christ* by Samuel Greene that lists 112 proofs. The best overall book on the subject is *Putting Jesus in His Place: The Case for the Deity of Christ* by Robert M. Bowman Jr. and J. Ed Komoszewski. I have included a list of other excellent books I recommend at the end.

I have generally quoted from the New King James Version of the Bible. Sometimes I use my own translation. Readers may want to consult other translations. They will find that most reputable translations substantiate the proofs in this volume. In keeping with the New King James Version, I have capitalized personal pronouns standing for both God and Jesus. After all, the purpose of this book is to show that Jesus is God.

I wish to thank Melody McNeill and Elizabeth Smith for their editorial help in preparing the manuscript for publication. I am grateful to the editorial staff of Reformation Heritage Books, especially Andrew Buss, Jay Collier, and David Woollin. Many thanks also go to Phil Johnson and others who gave useful comments on the manuscript. Any errors herein, however, are my own responsibility.

May the Lord of glory be pleased to bless this little book to help readers see the wonderful truth that Jesus Christ is indeed God.

JESUS IS

Explicitly Called God in John 1:1

This verse includes four words of one syllable each that clearly and profoundly teach the full deity of Jesus Christ: "The Word was God." It begins by saying that He existed "in the beginning." This is an echo of Genesis 1:1: "In the beginning God created the heavens and the earth." Next, the verb *was* in John 1:1 means "was," not "became." Thus, we could paraphrase it: "In the beginning of creation, the Word already was." Jesus existed before creation. Indeed, verse 3 says He created everything.

This "Word" is Jesus Christ, as seen later in verse 14: "The Word became flesh"—that is, became a human being. Revelation 19:13 says this is one of Christ's many names. This title refers to Him being the full and personal revelation of God.

Some erroneously translate the phrase as "The Word was a god," because the original Greek words do not use the word *the* before *God*. That is an incorrect translation. First, the word *God* does not always have *the* before it in Greek. Also, that translation would teach polytheism, in direct contradiction to the Bible's repeated teaching that there is only one God. All other gods are false gods (1 Cor. 8:5–6). If Jesus is only "a god," then He is a false god. Further, the Greek words use almost the exact same grammar as John 4:24: "God is Spirit." God is not "a spirit" among other equal spirits. Nor does it mean "Spirit is a god." It is also parallel to 1 John 4:8: "God is love," not "God is a love" or "Love is a god." Finally, John uses a certain grammar in which the subject and predicate are reversed to emphasize the nature of the subject—that is, "The Word really was by nature God."

This sets the tone for the rest of John's gospel, the theme of which is that Jesus Christ is indeed the Son of God with the same full deity as God the Father. Believing in Him means believing in who He truly is. The Word was and is God.

JESUS IS

Explicitly Called God in John 20:28

When Thomas was confronted by the risen Christ, he expressed his faith with the confession, "My Lord and my God!" From the lips of a Jew, this could only refer to the one true God Jehovah. It is similar to David's confession, "My God and my Lord" (Ps. 35:23), in which "Lord" is the holy name Jehovah. It is also similar to the greatest confession of the Old Testament: "The LORD our God, the LORD is one!" (Deut. 6:4). The Hebrew Bible has hundreds of places in which the two terms are used together, as in "Lord God" and "the Lord thy God." Thomas echoed Isaiah 25:1: "O LORD, You are my God." His double use of *my* implies he meant "my Lord God." If this is not a confession of faith that Jesus is Lord and God, then words have no meaning.

Some seek to avoid the obvious with far-fetched explanations. One says Thomas called Jesus "my Lord" but then looked up to heaven and called Jehovah "my God." But the text says, "Thomas answered and said to Him"—that is, Jesus. Another suggests that Thomas was so overcome with surprise that he took God's name in vain. But if that was true, then Jesus would have condemned him, not commended him. A person does not break one of the Ten Commandments at the moment of great faith while in the very presence of Jesus Christ Himself.

A third false idea is that Thomas was simply wrong. But the apostle John, who was present (John 20:26) and recorded this incident under the inspiration of the Holy Spirit, does not even hint that Thomas was in error. Jesus rebuked him for requiring a sign, not for his confession that Jesus was Lord and God. Those who say Thomas was wrong deny that Jesus is Lord and God. Such would include atheists and Muslims, for example. But they do not claim to be Christians. Nobody can legitimately claim to be a biblical Christian if he does not agree with Thomas's confession. To the true believer, Jesus Christ is "my Lord and my God."

JESUS IS

Explicitly Called God in Romans 9:5

This is another clear statement of the deity of Christ. He is called "the eternally blessed God." Paul states it under the inspiration of the Holy Spirit in the form of a burst of praise. Most major translations show this. Unfortunately, some tone it down and make it refer to God the Father in words such as, "Christ came. God who is over all be eternally blessed" (e.g., GNB, NEB, RSV). That is true, of course, but does not capture Paul's praise to Christ.

His words about Jesus Christ are similar to his opening words in Romans 1:3–4: "His Son Jesus Christ our Lord, who was born of the seed of David according to the flesh, and declared to be the Son of God with power." In both places, Paul states a profound truth. God promised to send the Messiah to the Jews. The Messiah would be a man born in the flesh as a Jew. Jesus was indeed physically a Jew. But the Messiah was also promised to be divine, God Himself in some mysterious way. In His humanity, Jesus was Jewish. The Gospels tell us He had a Jewish mother, Mary. But He was also the Son of God, for He did not have a human father. Romans 1:4 says He was "declared to be the Son of God." Romans 9:5 is even bolder. The one born of Jewish flesh is also "over all, the eternally blessed God." Paul then said, "Amen," and so should we.

JESUS IS

Explicitly Called God in 1 Timothy 3:16

Paul first says that this is a profound truth: "Without controversy great is the mystery of godliness." Sadly, the very truth he goes on to assert as "without controversy" has come to be disputed.

Several translations, such as the King James Version and the New King James Version, translate it as follows: "God was manifested in the flesh." This is the first of six short statements which may be a hymn or poem that Paul wrote or quoted. The rest of it clearly refers to Jesus. Jesus is God "manifested in the flesh." This fits in with other biblical passages that say Jesus "appeared" or "was manifested" (e.g., 1 John 3:5, 8).

Other translations choose to render 1 Timothy 3:16 as "He was manifested in the flesh" (e.g., ESV, HCSB). Some have *who* in the margin for *he*. The reason is that a few Greek manuscripts have *he* or *who* instead of *God*. The difference involves one or two Greek letters. The vast majority of Greek manuscripts, however, have *God*. But for the sake of argument, let's assume that either *he* or *who* is the true reading. If so, we must then ask, To whom does this refer? The closest antecedent is *God*, mentioned twice in verse 15. You would have to go all the way back to verse 13 to have it as Jesus Christ. In Greek, as in English, the closest antecedent is usually the correct one, especially if it is found twice in the same sentence. So, even if we go with *he* or *who*, the context still identifies the subject as God. God was manifested in the flesh.

To manifest means "to appear, display, show." If Jesus were only a man, it would be unnecessary to say, "He was manifested in the flesh," for how else could a person appear? Rather, manifestation implies something previously hidden. God is invisible (Col.

1:15). He chose to manifest Himself indirectly through creation, visions, dreams, and prophets and then personally and directly through Jesus Christ (Heb. 1:1–4). God appeared to us when He took on human flesh (see also John 1:14). Philippians 2:8 says, "Being found in appearance as a man, He humbled Himself." So 1 Timothy 3:16 fits in with the grand theme of the New Testament that God indeed was manifested in the flesh in the person of the Lord Jesus Christ.

JESUS IS

Explicitly Called God in Titus 2:13

This verse is strong enough to stand on its own, for it teaches that Jesus Christ is both "God and Savior." But lest anyone try to avoid it, we should examine the context.

Paul says much about God being the Savior in this short epistle. He refers to "God our Savior" in 1:3; 2:10; and 3:4. In 2:11 he says, "The grace of God that brings salvation has appeared to all men," and in 3:5 he adds, "According to His mercy He saved us." This is in keeping with the Bible's repeated assertions that God alone is our Savior. He saves us by grace. We do not save ourselves. But Paul also refers to "Jesus Christ our Savior" in Titus 1:4 and 3:6. There is only one Savior—Jesus who is God. And that's what Paul says in 2:13. Jesus is "our great God and Savior Jesus Christ." The grace of salvation has appeared (2:11). We await the second coming of the Savior one day (2:13).

This verse speaks of one Savior, not two. The Greek grammar is very clear on this. The terms *our great God* and *Savior* both refer to Jesus. Only one person is in view. We use a similar sentence structure ourselves, such as when a husband refers to "my darling and wife, Mary." Obviously, he isn't speaking of two different people. Mary is both his darling and his wife. Just so, Titus 2:13 says that Jesus Christ is both our "God and Savior." When He appears again one day, it will be clear to unbelievers that He is exactly who believers say He is—God.

JESUS IS

Explicitly Called God in Hebrews 1:8

This verse reads, "But to the Son He says: 'Your throne, O God, is forever and ever.'" It explicitly says that the Son is God and has an eternal throne. The entire chapter says that Jesus is greater than the angels and therefore must be God. Lest anyone think that Jesus is an angel or a created being higher than the angels, the author states that He is God.

Verses 5–13 contain a series of quotations from the Old Testament about the Son. We know that this Son is Jesus Christ. Several times the author prefaces his quotations with "He says" (vv. 6–7; cf. vv. 5, 13). Verse 8 has "He says" in italics, meaning the words are not in the Greek original but are a translational device to repeat the phrase from verses 6 and 7. But who is the "He" that is speaking? It is God the Father. These are the words of the Father about His Son. Thus, in verse 9 God the Father refers to Himself as "God, Your God." Jesus was God and was with God (John 1:1). In His humanity as Messiah, Jesus referred to the Father as "My God" (Matt. 27:46; John 20:17).

Those who still insist on denying Christ's deity sometimes twist Hebrews 1:8 to read "Your throne is God." But God is never the throne of a mere man. The whole idea is ludicrous, for a king is greater than his throne. The correct meaning is found in the Hebrew of Psalm 45:6–7, which is quoted here. Psalm 93:2 is indirectly alluded to as well. Both the Hebrew and Greek are plain: Jesus is explicitly called God, who has a throne that lasts forever and ever.

JESUS IS

Explicitly Called God in Hebrews 1:10

This great proof is often overlooked because it follows the over-whelmingly obvious assertion of Christ's deity in verse 8. But it develops the same truth. You could say that the author adds it to underscore his point, as if he repeated the fact by appealing to yet another Old Testament text.

He quotes Psalm 102:25: "Of old You laid the foundation of the earth, and the heavens are the work of Your hands." The Hebrew does not have the name Lord, but it is added in the book of Hebrews because the whole psalm is referring to the Lord, Jehovah (vv. 1, 12, 15, 16, 18, 19, 21, 22). He is "God" in verse 24. This is one of many Old Testament verses about the Lord God that are applied directly to the Lord Jesus in the New Testament (such as Isa. 29:13 in Matt. 15:7–9).

Hebrews 1:10–12 obviously is applied to "the Son" in keeping with verses 5–13. The Son is called "Lord"—that is, God. Further-more, what is said here plainly refers to acts and qualities that can be attributed to God alone. This Lord created the earth and the heavens (cf. Gen. 1:1). Creation will perish but not the Lord (Heb. 1:11), for this Lord is always the same (v. 12). The author later echoes this truth in Hebrews 13:8: "Jesus Christ is the same yes-terday, today, and forever." This unfailing and unchanged Creator is here explicitly identified as Jesus. Therefore, Jesus is explicitly called God because that is exactly who He is.

JESUS IS

Explicitly Called God in 2 Peter 1:1

Second Peter 1:1 speaks of "the righteousness of our God and Savior Jesus Christ." Elsewhere this ultimate righteousness refers to both God and Jesus, implying Jesus is God. God and Jesus are both said to be the only Savior (not *Saviors*), which supports the deity of Jesus. The only Savior saves from sin and gives us His righteousness.

The Greek syntax is the same as in Titus 2:13: "Our great God and Savior Jesus Christ." Notice that our text does not say, "Of our God and of our Savior Jesus Christ," which would imply two persons. That language is used in 2 Peter 1:2: "Of God and of Jesus our Lord." In that verse, the word *God* refers to the Father. These two verses together tell us that Jesus is God but not God the Father. Later, verse 11 says, "Of our Lord and Savior Jesus Christ," again applying both titles to Jesus. In 2 Peter, Jesus is often called "Lord" (1:2, 8, 14, 16; 2:1, 9). He is the "Lord and Savior" in 2:20; 3:2; and 3:18. *God* and *Lord* are surely interchangeable, as in the Old Testament in hundreds of places (see also 3:10, 12). Second Peter 1:1, then, plainly says that Jesus Christ is both God and Savior. The context and language demand it.

JESUS IS

Explicitly Called God in 1 John 5:20

The apostle John who so clearly and repeatedly showed in his gospel that Jesus is God did the same in his first epistle. He hints at it here and there (such as 2:22–23), but near the end he boldly affirms it in these words: He is "the true God and eternal life."

Occasionally a Bible translation misses the point, which is seized on by the unwary who would avoid the Bible's teaching on this vital doctrine. Some render this verse as "This is the true God and eternal life." The Greek pronoun could go either way. If, for the sake of argument, we went with the word *this* as the correct translation, that in itself does not deny Christ's deity. It could simply be saying that God who is the Father of Jesus is "the true God," which of course is true. That translation could also be taken to mean "This one"—that is, the one whom John has just mentioned. That would be "the Son of God...His Son Jesus Christ" in the first part of the verse. It could even be rendered, "This same one," referring to Jesus. But the best rendering is "He is the true God." The word *He* refers to Jesus Christ.

Incidentally, Jesus is here called eternal life, for we receive it from Him alone. We get righteousness from Jesus, for He is our righteousness (1 Cor. 1:30). The same is true with eternal life. This is the main theme of John's gospel (John 20:30–31). Finally, the meaning of 1 John 5:20 does not ultimately rest on whether we translate it as *He* or *this* but on what the pronoun refers to. The obvious antecedent is Jesus Christ, for He is mentioned twice in this very verse. John is plainly saying that Jesus is "the true God and eternal life."

JESUS IS

Explicitly Called "Mighty God"
in Isaiah 9:6

For centuries before Handel used this verse in his great oratorio, Christians had seen it as a wonderful prophecy of the birth of Jesus Christ. Isaiah 7:14 had predicted that Messiah would be born of a virgin, and later Isaiah 53 predicted that He would suffer and die for our sins. Isaiah 7:14 gave Him the name Immanuel. Here, He is given four additional names or titles that identify just who He is.

First, Jesus is "Wonderful, Counselor." Full of wonder and glory, only God is our great counselor—and no man can be counselor to God (Isa. 40:13; Rom. 11:34).

Second, He is called "Mighty God." This echoes the meaning of Isaiah 7:14: "God with us." This title is applied to Jesus in Revelation 1:8 when He is called "Almighty." By no legitimate exegesis could Isaiah 9:6 be translated "God is mighty," as if the title were only saying something about God the Father and not the Son who bears the name. The Son is "Mighty God." This name finds a parallel in Jeremiah 32:18: "The Great, the Mighty God, whose name is the LORD of hosts." Jehovah is also called "the Mighty God" in Isaiah 10:21 (cf. Deut. 10:17). Jesus is that same mighty God.

Third, He is called "Everlasting Father." This does not mean, as some think, that Jesus is the first person of the Trinity known as God the Father. Rather, as many Hebrew scholars point out, the words could be translated "Father of Eternity." There is also a sense in which Jesus is father to Christians (Heb. 2:13), though this is not the usual theological metaphor describing Christ's relation to His people. But either way, this third title attributes eternity to Jesus, which means He is God, for God alone is eternal.

The fourth title is "Prince of Peace," for Jesus made peace for us at the cross (Eph. 2:14) and gives us His peace (John 14:27). Those who believe Isaiah 9:6 can joyfully sing along with Handel's great oratorio of praise. Jesus is indeed the "Mighty God."

JESUS IS

Explicitly Called "God with Us"
in Matthew 1:23

Before Jesus was born, God sent an angel to announce what His name would be. Curiously, the angel said that this baby would have two names, though the rest of the New Testament refers to only one of them. That is the name Jesus, which means "Jehovah saves" (Matt. 1:21, 25). Does this not mean that Jesus is Jehovah come in the flesh to save us?

The angel also said that Jesus would be named Immanuel, referring to Isaiah 7:14. The Hebrew name means "God with us" (Matt. 1:23). Jesus is God with us. He is both Jehovah and God, with us to save us. The text does not say it means "God is with us," though that is true. It omits the *is* to identify the One being named. Who is the baby born at the first Christmas? He is "God with us."

Matthew 1:23 quotes Isaiah 7:14 and applies it to the virgin birth of Jesus. That, too, gives indisputable proof of Christ's deity. His mother was human; His Father was God. He had no human father or divine mother. A person receives his nature from his parents, as seen in the DNA code. Jesus had two natures, one human and one divine. These verses coincide with several others that teach the two natures of Jesus Christ in one person.

The glory of Christ's virgin-born incarnation is completely lost if we fail to see that He is God. If He were only a man, there would be no need for a virgin birth. Joseph could have been His father. But the Bible says everywhere that God was His Father. That virgin-born baby in the manger was indeed "God with us."

JESUS

Used the Divine Name I AM

When Moses asked God for His name, He replied, "I AM WHO I AM" (Ex. 3:14). The latter part of the verse shortens it to "I AM." God is the great I AM, the One who is, the self-sufficient and eternal Creator. The Hebrew term is incorporated into God's personal name, Yahweh, also popularly translated as Jehovah. It basically means the same as "I AM." This I AM is the one true God. "Now see that I, even I, am He" (Deut. 32:39). "I am He.... I, even I, am the LORD.... I am God" (Isa. 43:10–12; cf. 41:4, 13).

Now, Jesus Christ used the holy name I AM of Himself on several occasions and in various ways. Sometimes He said "I am" in such a way as to assert His full deity (see Matt. 14:27; Mark 14:62; John 4:26; 6:20, 35; 8:12, 23–24, 28, 58; 10:7, 9, 11, 14, 36; 11:25; 13:13, 19; 14:6; 15:1, 5; Rev. 1:8, 17–18; 2:23; 21:6; 22:13). Note John 18:5–8 says, "I am.... I am.... I have told you that I am." When asked by the high priest if He was the Christ, He replied, "I am" (Mark 14:62).

Jesus included the I AM name in His seven self-identifying sayings in the Gospel of John: "I am" the Bread of Life (6:35); the Light of the World (8:12); the Door (10:7); the Good Shepherd (10:11); the resurrection and the life (11:25); the way, the truth, and the life (14:6); and the true vine (15:1).

Most of these statements are found in the Gospel of John, the book of the Bible that most clearly and repeatedly sets forth Jesus as God. To read it and deny Jesus is God would be as foolhardy as to hear God in the burning bush say, "I AM," and deny that God is who He says He is. Only God can honestly say He is the great I AM.

JESUS SAID

He Is God in John 8:24

Here is an example of where Jesus explicitly used the divine name I AM of Himself. He said, "Therefore I say to you that you will die in your sins; for if you do not believe that I am, you will die in your sins" (author's paraphrase).

Some translations miss the point by rendering the words as "I am He." That would be a puzzle without an answer. Why would they die in their sins if they did not believe that Jesus was some unidentified "he"? He who? But there is no personal pronoun *he* in the Greek, and it is unnecessary to add it in the English translation. Jesus clearly meant what He said: "I AM," as in verse 58.

The point He made was awesomely holy. Jesus boldly announced that people will die lost in their sins if they fail to believe that He is the divine I AM. As John repeatedly says in his gospel, we are saved from our sins by believing in Jesus Christ, including believing the truth about who He is (e.g., 20:31). No faith—no salvation. John 8:24 is an echo of 3:36. Those who do not believe in Jesus Christ are still under the wrath of God.

John 8:25 clinches it: "Then they said to Him, 'Who are You?' And Jesus said to them, 'Just what I have been saying to you from the beginning.'" They asked Him what Moses asked God in Exodus 3:13. But unlike Moses, the Jews of John 8 did not believe in the I AM who spoke to them words of divine self-identification. The same goes for anyone today who does not believe that Jesus Christ is the one and only I AM—that is, Jehovah God.

JESUS SAID

He Is God in John 8:58

This is another time that Jesus explicitly used the divine name I AM of Himself. Throughout the chapter, He disputed with the Jews about God. They wrongly claimed to be children of Abraham (John 8:39). They were physically (v. 37) but not spiritually. In reality, they were children of the devil (v. 44). Abraham, the father of the Jews and an example of saving faith in the true God, believed in Jesus Christ (v. 56). When asked how Abraham could have believed in Jesus some two thousand years before Jesus was born, He straightforwardly answered, "Most assuredly, I say to you, before Abraham was, I AM" (v. 58).

Here Jesus explicitly said He lived before Abraham. At the least, that would mean He was over two thousand years old, more than twice as old as the oldest recorded man in biblical history. (Methuselah lived to be 969, according to Gen. 5:27.) But Jesus meant far more. He did not merely say, "I am older than Abraham" or "Before Abraham lived, I already was." Rather, He intentionally said, "I AM," the holy name of God of Exodus 3:14. God is eternal and lives in an eternal now (cf. Rev. 1:8). Note that Jesus did not say, "I am this" or "I am He." He said, "I AM," as God said in Exodus 3:14.

Notice how the Jews responded to this in John 8:59. They attempted to stone Jesus for blasphemy. God's holy law given to the Jews through Moses demanded execution for anyone who blasphemed God or incited idolatry of a false god. To falsely claim to be God would be the height of blasphemy and self-idolatry. The Jews again tried to stone Jesus for the same reason (John 10:33) and eventually succeeded in having Him executed by crucifixion.

Those who deny that Jesus is the great I AM are siding with the unbelieving Jews. In effect, they are agreeing with their verdict and the murder of Christ. Unbelief in Christ is akin to crucifying Him again (Heb. 6:6).

One more point bears mentioning. The grammar of John 8:58 is reminiscent of Psalm 90:2: "Before the mountains were brought forth, or ever You had formed the earth and the world, even from everlasting to everlasting, You are God." Note the present tense *are*. Before the world was created, God is. As Jesus said, "Before Abraham was, I AM."

JESUS SAID

He Is God in the Book of Revelation

In several parallel verses, Jesus claimed to be God in the last book of the Bible. First, Revelation 1:8 reads, "'I am the Alpha and the Omega, the Beginning and the End,' says the Lord, 'who is and who was and who is to come, the Almighty.'" This is another I AM saying in which Jesus used the divine name I AM of Himself (Ex. 3:14). *Alpha* and *omega* are the first and last letters of the Greek alphabet. The words "the Beginning and the End" are not in some ancient manuscripts and are thus omitted from some English translations, but they are used by Christ in Revelation 21:6 and 22:13. The meaning is the same in both phrases. He is the first Alpha and the last Omega. This is said by "the Lord." Some translations render it as "the Lord God," for only God could truthfully claim this for Himself. Then He says He is the eternal past, present, and future One. Last, in case anyone doubted who is speaking, He identifies Himself as "Almighty" (cf. Rev. 4:8).

Next, Revelation 1:11 says, "I am the Alpha and the Omega, the First and the Last." The second phrase parallels the first and is repeated in verse 17. Later, God says to John, "I am the Alpha and the Omega, the Beginning and the End" (21:6), and again, "I am the Alpha and the Omega, the Beginning and the End, the First and the Last" (22:13). The phrase "the Alpha and the Omega" is not in some manuscripts and translations in 22:13, but that does not seriously affect the meaning, for it has already been stated.

To get the force of these three parallel statements, we need to ask two questions. The first is, What do they mean? The obvious answer is that they refer to God as the one and only God. He is First and Last, with none other in between. This echoes several verses in Isaiah 40–48 where God mocks false gods: "I, the LORD, am the first; and with the last I am He" (41:4); "I am the First and I am the Last; besides Me there is no God" (44:6); "I am He, I am the First, I am also the Last" (48:12). There can be only one First and one Last; therefore, there is only one true God. Note that these words are spoken by Jehovah God. No angel or mere man dares speak such words.

The second question is, Who spoke these words in Revelation? First, Revelation 1:8 simply says "the Lord" (or "Lord God" in some translations). The speaker in 21:6 is identified in verse 5 as "He who sat on the throne." In Revelation, both God the Father and Jesus Christ sit on the throne together as one. Other places are more specific. The speaker of Revelation 1:11 is the one speaking like a trumpet (v. 10), whom John then identifies as Jesus (vv. 12–13). Next, the speaker in 2:8 is also Jesus, who is dictating the letters of chapters 2 and 3. Revelation 2:8 describes Him as "the First and the Last, who was dead, and came to life." That certainly is not the Father but Jesus Christ. Finally, the person in 22:13 is the same person who says in verse 12, "I am coming quickly"—namely, Jesus (cf. v. 20). He identifies Himself as "I, Jesus" in verse 16.

Put all these verses together in any combination, and the plain conclusion is the same. Jesus Christ explicitly said He is the Alpha and the Omega, the First and the Last, the Beginning and the End. Those are terms for the one true God. To deny this is as gross a sin as to believe the false gods that God mocked in Isaiah 40–48.

JESUS KNEW

That the Jews Understood His Claim to Be God

The unbelieving Jews attempted to kill Jesus on several occasions. The first was in Luke 4:29. John's gospel records three instances in which they tried to stone Jesus for claiming to be God (5:18; 8:59; 10:31). In 5:18, it was because He said God was His Father in a special way, "making Himself equal with God." In 8:59, it was because Jesus said in verse 58, "Before Abraham was, I AM." In 10:31, it was because He used the I AM name again (vv. 7, 9, 11, 14) and claimed God as His Father (vv. 15, 17, 18, 25, 29, 32), specifically when He said, "I and My Father are one" (v. 30) and claimed to be the Son of God (v. 36).

Some thought Jesus was insane or demon-possessed for making such claims (10:19–20), but the majority accused Him of blasphemy: "For a good work we do not stone You, but for blasphemy, and because You, being a Man, make Yourself God" (10:33; cf. 7:30, 44; 10:39).

Now the law of God given through Moses commanded that a person who blasphemed God should be put to death (Lev. 24:16). That would include claiming to be God, as the Jews rightly surmised. If Jesus were not God as He claimed, then the Jews would have been justified in trying to stone Him. We would applaud the crucifixion for the same reason. Jesus would have gotten what He deserved as a blaspheming Jew. But nobody who claims to be a Christian ever defends the crucifixion. Jesus was innocent of all charges, including the charge of blasphemy.

Why? Because Jesus really is who He said He is. He is the Son of God, with God the Father as His Father in a unique way, the I AM who is equal with the Father and is God Himself. The

Jews were wrong to disbelieve Him but not wrong in understanding His claims to deity. Those today who deny that Jesus is God must attempt to deny that Jesus ever claimed deity or must prove that the Jews misunderstood Jesus on three occasions. Both would be futile, for John's gospel records these events to illustrate his theme that Jesus was indeed who He claimed to be—God in the flesh. Note that Jesus did not deny their charge of His claiming to be God; He only said that they were wrong to charge Him with blasphemy.

The unbelieving Jews murdered an innocent man. It never seemed to occur to most of them that Jesus Christ might actually have been who He said He was. Many people today—Jew and Gentile—make the same mistake and do not properly search the Scriptures for verification of Christ's claims. But by God's grace, others then and now believe that Jesus was right. Rather than deny or attack His claim to deity, they fall at His feet in faith and worship.

We might add that Mormons also misunderstand Jesus's claims, such as His words in John 10:34–36. They mistakenly think that Jesus was a man who became a god and that Mormons can become gods as well. But the truth is that Jesus was not a man who became a god but rather God who became the God-man. No mere man can become a god (Gen. 3:5). Jesus is, was, and always will be God. That's truth, not blasphemy. It is blasphemy to deny it.

JESUS IS LORD

The proper name for God in Hebrew is Yahweh, sometimes incorrectly spelled Jehovah. It is usually translated into English as LORD (all capital letters). The greatest theological statement in the Old Testament is Deuteronomy 6:4: "The LORD our God, the LORD is one!" Other verses say much the same thing: "The LORD, He is God!" (1 Kings 18:39); There is no "God" but "the LORD" (cf. Ps. 18:31; Isa. 45:5–6, 14, 18, 21; 46:9); "God is the LORD" (Ps. 118:27); "You, whose name alone is the LORD, are the Most High" (Ps. 83:18).

When the Jews translated the Hebrew Bible into Greek, they usually translated the Hebrew word *Yahweh* by the Greek word *Kurios*, meaning "Lord." Greek-speaking Jews used *Kurios* when referring to God and often refrained from speaking the Hebrew name Yahweh. *Kurios* is the most popular name for God in the Greek New Testament. But it is also the most common title for Jesus Christ. He is called Lord, Lord Jesus, the Lord Christ, the Lord Jesus Christ, and such terms many, many times. One of the earliest Christian confessions of faith was "Jesus is Lord" (1 Cor. 12:3; cf. 2 Cor. 4:5; Phil. 2:11). He is "the Lord of glory" (1 Cor. 2:8; James 2:1) and "the Lord from heaven" (1 Cor. 15:47). There is only "one Lord Jesus Christ" (1 Cor. 8:6; cf. Eph. 4:5). Thomas called Jesus "my Lord and my God" (John 20:28). Jesus said, "You call Me Teacher and Lord, and you say well, for so I am" (John 13:13, another possible I AM statement).

To say "Jesus is Lord" is to say "Jesus is God." The Yahweh/Jehovah of the Old Testament is the Jesus of the New Testament. The very name Jesus means "Yahweh saves" (Matt. 1:21). The fundamental creed of the Old Testament, "The LORD our God, the LORD is one," is the same as the basic creed of the New Testament, "Jesus Christ is Lord." To deny that Jesus is the same Lord is to deny that Yahweh is the one true God.

JESUS IS
Lord of All

There is only one God. Atheists say there is no God, pantheists say all is God, dualists say there are two gods, and polytheists say there are many gods. They are all wrong. The one true God reigns over everything. The Creator is Lord over His creation. He has full authority over everything and everyone. If God is not Lord of all, He is not Lord at all. The very definition of God says so.

The Bible says the same thing about Jesus Christ: "The same Lord over all" (Rom. 10:12). He is Lord over Jew and Gentile, men and women, rich and poor, all without exception. He is "Lord of both the dead and the living" (Rom. 14:9). Jesus is Lord over all humans who have ever lived or who will ever live, even those who are now dead. Acts 10:36 says, "Jesus Christ—He is Lord of all." He is transcendently exalted over everything (John 3:31; Rom. 9:5; Eph. 1:20–21; Phil. 2:9).

There cannot be two Lords of all, otherwise each would not be the Lord over the other. That is the self-contradiction of dualist religions such as Zoroastrianism and the cosmic dualism of Tao-ism. There is and can be only one ultimate Lord of all. Similarly, each human can submit to only one Lord, not two, otherwise he will sooner or later serve only one (Matt. 6:24; cf. 1 Kings 18:21). The fact that the Bible says "Jesus is Lord of all" is clear proof that He is God of all.

JESUS IS
Lord of Lords

Jesus is called "Lord of lords" in three places (1 Tim. 6:15; Rev. 17:14; 19:16). This is an emphatic way of saying that He is ultimate Lord. It is taken from the Old Testament worship of the one true God, especially Deuteronomy 10:17: "The LORD your God is God of gods and Lord of lords, the great God, mighty and awesome" (see also Ps. 136:2–3; Dan. 2:47; 11:36). The term *Lord of lords* is equivalent to *God of gods*, for the Lord is God. It does not mean there are actually other gods in existence. Other gods are demons and idols (1 Cor. 10:20), and the one true God is infinitely above them.

In Hebrew, something is described as superlative in this way— for example, vanity of vanities, song of songs, holy of holies. Even in English we say "wonder of wonders," meaning the greatest wonder. *Lord of lords* means the greatest Lord, the superlative Lord, the infinitely highest Lord. Paul and John would never have dared call Jesus "Lord of lords" if they believed He was only a man and not God.

Jesus is Lord of lords, and therefore He is God of gods, for both terms mean the same thing. Jesus is not a mere god; He is God. He is God over all gods. He is the ultimate Lord and God.

JESUS IS
King of Kings

Jesus is also called "King of kings" in 1 Timothy 6:15, Revelation 17:14, and 19:16. He is called "Lord of lords" in these same places, for both terms mean the same thing. Both are used of God, the God of gods and ultimate King and Lord. "King of kings" is basically the same as "Lord of kings" (Dan. 2:47) and "ruler over the kings of the earth" (Rev. 1:5). In these places, Jesus is not only the superlative King but ruler over all earthly kings. Human kings have authority over other humans, but Jesus has authority over all human kings as well as queens, princes, presidents, pharaohs, caesars, prime ministers, generals, and dictators.

Back in the mid-twentieth century, the shah of Iran took on himself the title "King of Kings." He was later forced to leave office and flee for his life. That will never happen to the true King of kings, Jesus Christ. He was never elected, nor did He seize power in a revolution or coup. He is King of kings first by divine right and second in His humanity as reward for His messianic work on the cross.

All men are already His subjects, whether they know it or not, whether they like it or not. His kingship is not dependent on their submission or vote. True Christians are those who willingly and gratefully submit to His kingship. We delight in having Christ as our king. Unconverted sinners refuse to submit (Luke 19:14), but Christians count it their highest privilege to have Christ as their absolute King. Better to be His subject than to be the king of an empire. Unconverted sinners will eventually be punished as wicked rebels (Luke 19:27). Some lost sinners pretend to be His servants. Others admit they are not His servants. Then there are those who say they have Christ as Savior but not as King. Still others falsely claim to be Christians but deny that Jesus is God. But in truth, Jesus Christ is still the King of kings who will reward His followers and punish His enemies.

JESUS IS

the Lord and King of Glory

The Bible links the ideas of Lord and King and attributes them both to Jesus: He is the Lord and King of glory. Psalm 24 says, "Who is this King of glory? The LORD strong and mighty…. The LORD of hosts, He is the King of glory" (vv. 8, 10). Note the word *the*. God is the only King of glory. Also, the Hebrew text uses the holy name Yahweh, LORD, of this divine king. God is the glorious King who has all glory in Himself.

Twice in the New Testament, Jesus is called "the Lord of glory" (1 Cor. 2:8; James 2:1). This is the same basic term as *King of glory*, for the Greek words for *Lord* and *king* are basically synonymous, as they are in Hebrew. It would be extreme quibbling to say that God is the King of glory but Jesus is the Lord of glory—as if God is not the Lord of glory or Jesus is not the King of glory. The New Testament further uses the term *God of glory* with reference to God (Acts 7:2) even as Psalm 29:3 does. Jesus and the Father shared divine glory in eternity before Christ became a man (John 17:5). There is an infinite and eternal glory within the Trinity. The God of glory created all things to display His glory specifically to the elect. God shows but does not share this glory (Isa. 42:8; 48:11). Since God alone is the King and Lord of glory, and Jesus is also King and Lord of glory, it necessarily follows that Jesus Christ is God.

JESUS IS

Equal to God the Father

Philippians 2:6 says that Jesus, "being in the form of God, did not consider it robbery to be equal with God." The Jews sought to stone Jesus when they heard Him call God His Father. They knew this was a claim to be "equal with God" (John 5:18).

But who can be equal to God except God (Isa. 40:25)? God is infinite—who but another infinite being could be equal with infinity? God alone is also eternal—who but God could be equal to the eternal God? The question is answered in John 1:1. Jesus is God and is with God. Each member of the Trinity is equal with the others. There is no subordination of being within the Trinity. There is only one God, but each of the three members of the Trinity is God, is with God, and is equal in power and glory with the others. The Son is equal with the Father (Phil. 2:6). The Spirit is as well. And the Son is also equal with the Spirit.

Someone may ask, "But didn't Jesus say, 'My Father is greater than I'?" (John 14:28). Yes, He did. In His humanity, He was in a state of humility to the Father, but in His deity, He was equal with the Father. Humanity, even the glorified humanity of Christ that was united with His deity in the incarnation, is not equal in being with deity. This brings us to the threshold of two of the greatest biblical mysteries of all: the Trinity and the dual natures of Christ. The mystery is not resolved by denying Christ's deity, let alone His humanity. Rather, we must ponder them in holy wonder and worship Him as God.

JESUS

Has All the Fullness of God

Paul wrote the epistle to the Colossians to warn them about certain Gnostic heretics who denied the full deity of Jesus. They admitted that He was no mere man but said He was something like an angel. They called Him an *archon*, something like the ray of light that emanates from the sun but is not the sun itself. This is similar to the idea today that says Jesus has more divinity in Him than we do but is still not fully God. Both views say that only God the Father has the "fullness of deity."

Paul refuted this error by saying, "In Him dwells all the fullness of the Godhead bodily (Col. 2:9; see also 1:19). Note the word *fullness*. Jesus Christ is fully God, not partly God. Only God can contain the fullness of God. Just as you cannot put the entire ocean in a teacup, so the complete fullness of deity cannot be put into a mere man or angel. Infinity cannot be contained fully in a finite thing. Jesus has the capacity, however, for He is God. Only God can contain God.

JESUS IS

the Second Person of the Trinity

The deity of Jesus Christ is inseparably related to the Bible's teaching on the Trinity, which is summed up in three points. First, there is only one God (Isa. 45:5–6, 14, 18, 21; 46:9; 1 Tim. 1:17; 2:5; and many more). Second, the Father is God (1 Cor. 1:3; 8:6; 2 Cor. 1:2; Eph. 1:2–3; 3:14), the Son is God, and the Holy Spirit is God (Ps. 51:11; Acts 5:3–4; 1 Cor. 6:11; 2 Cor. 3:17–18). Third, the Father is not the Son (John 14:28), the Son is not the Spirit (John 14:26), and the Spirit is not the Father (John 14:26). For example, Jesus prayed to the Father, not to Himself. The Son, not the Father or the Spirit, died on the cross. The Spirit, not the Father or the Son, came on the day of Pentecost.

Matthew 28:19 is the classic verse that lists the Trinity: "In the name of the Father and of the Son and of the Holy Spirit." All three are mentioned together multiple times in the Bible (cf. Isa. 48:16; 61:1; Zech. 12:10; Matt. 3:16–17; Mark 1:10–11; Luke 1:35; 3:21–22; John 3:34–36; 14:16, 26; 16:13–15; Acts 2:33, 38–39; Rom. 8 [whole chapter]; 15:16, 30; 2 Cor. 13:14; Gal. 4:6; Eph. 1:3–14, 17; 2:18; 3:14–16; 4:4–6; 1 Thess. 1:2–5; 2 Thess. 2:13–14; 1 Peter 1:2; 1 John 5:8–9). Also, the Hebrew word *Elohim* (God) is plural yet used with a singular verb (e.g., Deut. 6:4, which emphasizes that there is only one God). God speaks of Himself as "We" and "Us" in Genesis 1:26; 3:22; 11:7; and Isaiah 6:8. There is both unity and diversity in God.

The differences between the three persons (or members) are these. The Father eternally begets the Son and with the Son sends the Spirit. Yet the Father is neither begotten nor sent. The Son is begotten by the Father and does not beget, and with the Father sends the Spirit. The Spirit is not begotten but proceeds from the Father and the Son. (See John 1:14, 18; 3:16–18; 14:16; 15:26; Rev. 22:1.) Therefore, there is one God who eternally exists in three persons. Each is God and with God (John 1:1).

True Christians firmly believe in the Trinity but equally firmly deny that there are three gods. Muslims, Jehovah's Witnesses, and Jews are wrong to accuse us of tritheism. There is only one true God, not three. But within the one true God are three distinct members—that is, the Father, the Son, and the Holy Spirit (Matt. 28:19).

JESUS
Has a Unique Relationship with God the Father

Jesus has a relationship with the Father unlike anyone else. No human or angel has ever had or ever will have such a relationship. It speaks of His deity. He is God and with God (John 1:1), God face-to-face with God. Jesus said, "I and My Father are one" (John 10:30), which the Jews rightly understood as claiming to be God (v. 33). He also said, "The Father is in Me, and I in Him" (John 10:38; cf. 14:10–11). Much of John 13 to 16 dwells on this theme, and virtually every verse of chapter 17 does as well. (See also Matt. 11:27; John 3:35; 5:19–27; 6:27; 8:18–19; 1 John 2:22–24; and 2 John 1:9.)

The Father and the Son are more deeply related than any human father and son. For example, a human father existed before his son was born, but Jesus is as eternal as the Father. This relationship is also closer than even that of a husband and wife, the deepest of all human relationships (Eph. 5:31). A husband and wife are one only in relationship, not in essence. Yet the Father and Son are one in divine essence as well as perfect and eternal in the relationship of their persons. This is the wonderful nature of the Trinity.

As John 17 indicates, Jesus's relationship with the Father did not begin when He was born. He had a relationship with the Father in eternity past, before the world began. They also had this relationship with the Holy Spirit within the Trinity. These interrelated relationships not only describe the Trinity but prove the deity of Christ.

Colossians 2:2 in some translations (e.g., NJKV) reads, "The mystery of God, both of the Father and of Christ." Some translations omit "both of the Father and of," but the fuller words are in the vast majority of Greek manuscripts. The meaning is "the mystery of God, including the Father who is God and Christ who is God." This clearly places Jesus Christ in the Godhead with the Father.

The relationship is also seen in the honor that is to be given to both of them. God alone is to be given ultimate honor (Rev. 4:9–11; 7:12; 19:1). But Jesus said, "All should honor the Son just as they honor the Father. He who does not honor the Son does not honor the Father who sent Him" (John 5:23). One cannot honor the Father as God if He does not honor the Son as God. To deny Christ's deity is to dishonor Him (John 8:49). True faith gives honor to Christ (1 Tim. 6:16; Rev. 5:12–13), for true believers worship both the Father and the Son.

JESUS IS

the Special Love of the Father

When Jesus was baptized, the Father said, "This is My beloved Son, in whom I am well pleased" (Matt. 3:17; see also Mark 1:11; Luke 3:22; 2 Peter 1:17). Jesus is "the Beloved" (Eph. 1:6) and "the Son of His love" (Col. 1:13) in whom the Father delighted from all eternity (Prov. 8:30). "The Father loves the Son" (John 5:20; cf. 10:17; 17:23). And of course, the Son has loved the Father from all eternity (John 14:31).

This great truth helps explain the Trinity. "God is love" (1 John 4:8, 16). That refers to God in His eternal being, not just in relation to us. God was love before there was anyone else to love except Himself. He loved Himself before He created angels and humans. Love must have both a subject and an object—a lover and a beloved. The Father eternally loved the Son, who eternally loved the Father. Jesus prayed, "You loved Me before the foundation of the world" (John 17:24). Undoubtedly the Holy Spirit was also involved in this eternal trinitarian love. Unless Jesus is a member of the eternal Trinity, the phrase "God is love" has no meaning. If the Father loved the Son before anything was created, then it follows that the Son is as eternally divine and uncreated as the Father.

Similarly, "the love of God" (Rom. 8:39) is equated with "the love of Christ" (Rom. 8:35). It is "the love of God which is in Christ Jesus our Lord" (v. 39). God is love and chose to let His eternal, internal love overflow to created beings. It comes to them through Jesus Christ. Jesus, then, is both the special object of the Father's love and the conduit by which it comes to us. That can only be said of one who is God.

JESUS

Sent the Holy Spirit

On the night before He died, Jesus promised to send the Holy Spirit (John 14:16; 15:26; 16:7; cf. Luke 24:49; Acts 1:5, 8). This was fulfilled on the day of Pentecost when the Spirit was sent from heaven following the glorious ascension of Jesus to heaven (Acts 2:33). Yet the Bible also says very clearly that only God can send the Holy Spirit (Isa. 40:13). He is "the gift of God" (Acts 8:15–20). The Spirit, being God, goes where He wishes, in perfect agreement with the Father and the Son (John 3:8). No mere man or angel has authority to send the Spirit.

In Joel 2:28 and Zechariah 12:10, God promised to pour out the Holy Spirit on His people. This was fulfilled in Acts 2. This was the baptism of the Holy Spirit (Acts 1:5), as predicted by John the Baptist (Matt. 3:11; Mark 1:8; Luke 3:16; John 1:33). Jesus baptized with the Holy Spirit, not with water. Note the Trinity in both the water baptism of Jesus and the Spirit baptism by Jesus.

God alone is the "fountain of living waters" (Jer. 2:13; 17:13). Jesus gives the water of life, living water, which is the Holy Spirit (John 4:10; 7:38–39; Rev. 21:6; 22:1). Since God alone can give the Spirit, this once more proves that Jesus Christ is God.

The Holy Spirit's ministry has several functions that bear on Christ's deity. He glorifies Jesus (John 16:14) and moves men to confess that "Jesus is Lord" (1 Cor. 12:3). The Holy Spirit would never do this for a mere man. The Holy Spirit is Himself God and does all this as part of God's great plan of glory. Jesus and the Spirit are both fully God and are sent into the world to reveal God's glory to us. Jesus, not the Spirit, is the focal point. The Spirit directs our full attention to Jesus as the ultimate and glorious revelation of God. To deny that Jesus is God is to be spiritually blind to this wonderful work of the Spirit.

JESUS IS

the Perfect Revelation of God

God is invisible to us at present (1 Tim. 1:17). Those in heaven see Him, and the day will come when He will be visible to all Christians. But meanwhile, God hides Himself, as it were (Isa. 45:15). Nobody can see God directly and live.

God revealed things about Himself indirectly and gradually through visions, dreams, voices, miracles, and Scripture (Heb. 1:1–4). Those were but impersonal shadows. But in the fullness of time, God revealed Himself directly and personally through Jesus Christ. Jesus said, "He who has seen Me has seen the Father" (John 14:9). To see Jesus is to see God. "He is the image of the invisible God" (Col. 1:15; cf. 2 Cor. 4:4). Jesus is not a shadowy or partial revelation, but He is "the brightness of His glory and the express image of His person" (Heb. 1:3). Jesus showed what no man had ever or could ever see in this life—God Himself. "No one has seen God at any time. The only begotten Son, who is in the bosom of the Father, He has declared Him" (John 1:18). That could never be said of any mere man, let alone an angel.

No picture is the perfect image of the person it portrays. The Bible says that man was created in the image of God (Gen. 1:26), but that image is now marred by sin. However, Jesus is not merely "in the image of God." He is the very image of God Himself (Col. 1:15). He is the perfect personal revelation of God Himself. Only God can be the perfect revelation of God; therefore, Jesus is God.

JESUS IS
the Only Way to God

There is only one God and only one way to God—God's way. All of man's ways lead to death and hell (Prov. 14:12; Matt. 7:13). Only God can provide the way to Himself, and He does it by bridging the gap between Himself and man. Jesus is that bridge. Because He is both God and man, He is therefore uniquely the way to God (1 Tim. 2:5). The only time God became a man was when Jesus came to earth and He is the only man who has ever been God incarnate.

Jesus said, "I am the way, the truth, and the life. No one comes to the Father except through Me" (John 14:6) and "I am the door" (John 10:7, 9). Nobody knows God personally unless Jesus chooses to reveal Himself to him (Matt. 11:27). There is no salvation except through Jesus Christ (Acts 4:12). Could any of this possibly be said of a mere man, even a sinless man (of which there are none)? Of course not.

To deny that Jesus is God would logically imply several errors: that there is no God, or that there is no way to God, or that there are many ways to God, or that we make our own way to God. The deity of Christ sweeps those errors aside and proves them to be false ways that end only in hell. Christ is the only way to God because He is the only God.

JESUS IS

the Creator of the Universe

The universe was created by God, not self-created by evolution. "In the beginning God created the heavens and the earth" (Gen. 1:1). He created the universe out of nothing by simply speaking it into existence (Gen. 1; Heb. 11:3). Only God has such power, and only God existed before the creation of the universe. God created the angels before He created the physical part of the universe (Job 38:4–7), but before that there was only God. God alone is the Creator (e.g., Pss. 95:6–7; 102:25; Isa. 40:28; 44:24; Heb. 1:10; 3:4; 11:3; Rev. 4:11).

The Bible also teaches that Jesus Christ is the Creator of all (John 1:2–3, 10; 1 Cor. 8:6; Col. 1:16; Heb. 1:2, 10; Rev. 3:14). Jesus is not a created being but rather the uncreated Creator. This refers to His eternal divine being, of course, for His human body and soul were indeed created. Since Jesus created all things, in a marvelous way He created His own humanity.

It is quite incorrect to suggest, as some do, that Jesus merely created "all other things," as if God first created Jesus, then Jesus created everything else. That's not what the Bible says. Rather, Jesus was a member of the holy Trinity involved in original creation with the Father and the Spirit. God created the world "through Jesus" and "for Him" (Eph. 3:9; Col. 1:16). Proverbs 16:4 says, "The LORD has made all for Himself." God created the universe and then personally stepped into it in the person of Jesus Christ. The Creator became part of the creation, as it were. This awesome truth glorifies God greatly. Reject Christ's deity, and it is lost.

JESUS

Sustains the Universe

After God created the universe out of nothing, He rested from all His work (Gen. 1:31–2:2) but has continued to sustain His creation and guide it (Neh. 9:6). We call this *providence*. God provides for His universe. He feeds the animals, He gives life to all, and He provides happiness.

God does all this through the Lord Jesus Christ. "In Him all things consist," or hold together (Col. 1:17). Jesus upholds and guides the universe (Heb. 1:3). God alone does this (Neh. 9:6), so this clearly teaches that Jesus Christ is God. Jesus was doing this before, during, and after He was on earth in the flesh. Angels are used by God sometimes in affecting the world but only in limited ways at best. Only the infinite and omnipotent God can sustain the whole universe. The universe itself is not infinite—only God is infinite, and the Creator is infinitely greater than the creation (1 Kings 8:27). Obviously, then, only God who is infinite in being and power could sustain the universe. Jesus is just that.

JESUS

Is Eternal

God alone is eternal. He has always existed. He is from everlasting to everlasting (Ps. 90:2). His very name, Yahweh (Jehovah), means "I AM" and implies an "eternal now" being. He has no beginning or end. The eternity of God is taught in Deuteronomy 33:27; Psalm 93:2; Isaiah 57:15; and 1 Timothy 1:17, among other places. He not only fills all time but existed "before time began" (2 Tim. 1:9). God created time and is not limited by it. He is "the eternal God" (Deut. 33:27).

Does not the Bible say the same about Jesus Christ? Indeed, it does. He is described as being eternal many times (Isa. 9:6; Mic. 5:2 [cf. Matt. 2:5–6]; John 1:1, 15; 8:58; 17:5; Eph. 1:4; Col. 1:17; 2 Tim. 1:9; Heb. 1:12; 13:8; Rev. 1:8, 18; 5:14; 22:13). In His humanity He had a birth day, but He already had existed before He was born. His deity had no beginning but was from everlasting. He lived before the angels were made, for He created them. He existed before all creation, for He is the Creator of all.

Jesus possesses all the divine attributes that only God has. No mere man is eternal, infinite, or immutable. Scripture specifically calls our attention to the eternity of Christ. We would do well to ponder and believe it.

JESUS

Is Unchangeable

Immutability is another attribute that only God has. "I am the LORD, I do not change" (Mal. 3:6). He never changes in His perfect being (Ps. 102:27; James 1:17). God is not growing in His being or developing in His essence. Change would be for the better or worse, but God is already absolutely perfect. The universe changes; God does not (Ps. 102:25–27). The world is affected by sin and is degenerating, but God is holy and not subject to decay.

The same Bible also says that Jesus Christ is unchangeable. Hebrews 13:8 says, "Jesus Christ is the same yesterday, today, and forever." Hebrews 1:12, quoting Psalm 102:27, explicitly speaks about God and applies it to Jesus Christ: "You are the same, and Your years will not fail." Jesus grew and changed in His humanity (Luke 2:40), for humanity as such is not immutable. Humans grow. Even in heaven we will grow in knowledge and love. But in His deity, Christ has never changed. Why? Because He is and always will be God.

JESUS

Is Omnipresent

God's omnipresence means He is everywhere; there is no place where God is absent. He is infinite. He is greater than the universe and cannot be contained by it (1 Kings 8:27). His omnipresence is taught in 2 Chronicles 2:6; 6:18; Psalm 139:7–12; Jeremiah 23:24; and elsewhere. This does not mean that the universe is God (pantheism) or that the universe is part of God (panentheism). The Creator is not the creation (Rom. 1:25). Rather, God is everywhere but is not everything. He is near to us all (Acts 17:27).

Even so with Jesus. He "fills all in all" (Eph. 1:23; cf. 4:10). He is able to be with Christians all over the world at the same time (Matt. 18:20; 28:20). That is true only because He is God.

Of course, this applies only to Christ's deity, not His humanity. Jesus moved from place to place when He was on earth. He ascended from earth to heaven. He is not here on earth now in His body or soul. Historic Lutheranism teaches the strange theory which says that Christ now is "ubiquitous," or omnipresent in His glorified humanity. But the angel said to the women on resurrection morning, "He is not here" (Matt. 28:6). Humanity is necessarily limited to one place at a time. But deity is not limited, and in His deity, Christ is capable of being everywhere.

JESUS IS

Omniscient

God knows all things—everything that was, is, or ever will be. He knows things that never will be; He knows all possibilities (Matt. 11:21, 23). God does not learn, for He already knows everything. Nor does He forget, for He is "perfect in knowledge" (Job 36:4). "His understanding is infinite" (Ps. 147:5).

The same applies to Jesus Christ. He knows everything, even our secret thoughts (Matt. 9:4; 12:25; Mark 2:8; Luke 5:22; 6:8; 9:47; John 2:24–25; 4:29; 6:64; 16:30; 21:17; Rev. 2:23). Matthew 6:29 is an interesting example. Jesus said that Solomon was not clothed as beautifully as the flowers of the field. How did Jesus know this? Solomon lived almost a thousand years earlier. There were no photographs of him. He knew because He is everywhere and knows everything.

Some unbelievers point to Mark 13:32 and say that Jesus did not know the date of the second coming, as only God knows. The answer is quite simple yet profound. In His humanity, Jesus did not know everything. He grew in knowledge like the rest of us (Luke 2:40). Not so in His deity. It has not been revealed to us in Scripture how Jesus could be omniscient in His deity but not in His humanity, but this is part of the glorious mystery of the hypostatic union of two natures in one person.

Mere humans are never omniscient. Even glorified Christians in heaven will never know everything, for God alone is omniscient. But since Jesus knows everything, this proves that He is God.

JESUS IS

Omnipotent

This is another divine attribute that belongs to God alone. Being the Creator, He merely spoke the universe into being by divine permission and "the word of His power" (Heb. 1:3; see also Gen. 1). He has infinite power within Himself. He controls the entire cosmos. He never gets tired or sleepy (Ps. 121:4; Isa. 40:28). "Is anything too hard for the LORD?" (Gen. 18:14). He is God Almighty (Rev. 1:8) and can do whatever He wishes. The omnipotence of God is taught in Job 42:2; Jeremiah 32:17, 27; Matthew 19:26; Mark 10:27; Luke 1:37; 18:27; and elsewhere.

We should not be surprised to learn that, once more, a unique divine quality of God is attributed to Jesus Christ. He is omnipotent. He is "Almighty" (Rev. 1:8), the "Mighty God" (Isa. 9:6), and the "only Potentate" (1 Tim. 6:15). He has all authority (Matt. 28:18) and all power, therefore, He is omnipotent (Matt. 8:27; Phil. 3:21; 2 Peter 1:16). He sustains the universe by this power (Col. 1:17).

Jesus did not work miracles by power given to Him, as was the case with the prophets and apostles (Luke 9:1). He did them by His own power, together with the Father and the Spirit. He is infinitely more powerful than angels or humans. Angels are "mighty" (2 Thess. 1:7); Jesus is almighty. In worship, we recognize and attribute power to Jesus (1 Tim. 6:15; Rev. 5:12–13). The omnipotence of Christ is another glorious proof of His deity.

JESUS IS
Holy

Of all the attributes of God, none is more important than holiness. He is the "Holy One" (Pss. 71:22; 78:41; 89:18; Isa. 1:4; 31:1; 41:14; 43:3; 54:5; Hab. 3:3). "No one is holy like the LORD" (1 Sam. 2:2). The angels worship and sing, "Holy, holy, holy is the LORD of hosts" (Isa. 6:3; cf. Rev. 4:8). God is absolute holiness itself—light without even the smallest taint of darkness (1 John 1:5). Revelation says of Him, "You alone are holy" (Rev. 15:4).

Jesus Christ is also called the "Holy One" (Mark 1:24; Luke 4:34; Acts 2:27; 13:35, quoting Ps. 16:10). He never sinned. He could not sin, for He was impeccably holy. (See Isa. 53:9; Luke 1:35; 23:41; John 8:46; 14:30; Acts 2:27; 3:14; 4:27, 30; 13:35; 2 Cor. 5:21; Heb. 1:9; 4:15; 7:26; 9:14; 1 Peter 1:19; 2:22; 1 John 3:5; Rev. 3:7.) Though He could be tempted as man, He could not sin, because He was God, who cannot be tempted and cannot sin (James 1:13).

All mere men have sinned (Rom. 3:23; 5:12). Adam was created sinless but fell into sin. Jesus is the only exception to universal human sinfulness because He was also God—the holy God-man. His holy deity controlled and protected His sinless humanity in such a way that He never did or could sin. In this He is the second Adam who was greater than the first Adam.

Even angels can sin. Many did. The unfallen angels were protected from sinning by God's elective purpose (1 Tim. 5:21). But it was different with Jesus, for He is not an angel. He became a man lower than the angels (Heb. 2:9) but was superior to them. He has inherent holiness; they have derivative holiness. Jesus was absolutely holy, and this proves beyond doubt that He is God.

JESUS IS
the God of Truth

God is the true God (Jer. 10:10). He not only speaks the truth but is the truth. He cannot lie (Titus 1:2). He is the "God of truth" (Ps. 31:5; Isa. 65:16). Ultimate truth is not relative or absolute. It is not a principle but a person—the Lord Jesus is the God of truth. He is "the true God" (1 John 5:20) who said, "I am the way, the truth, and the life" (John 14:6). Pilate asked Jesus, "What is truth?" (John 18:38), yet the Truth Himself was right in front of him. Jesus spoke the truth when He claimed to be God. He was not merely a good teacher, as some believe. Good teachers do not falsely claim to be God. If He were not God, then we could dismiss Him as a bad man, a lunatic, or a demon-possessed man, and we certainly would not honor Him as a good teacher. But He is who He said He is, so we embrace Him as more than a good teacher of truth—we worship Him as the God of truth.

JESUS IS
the Good God

We frequently read in the Bible that "the LORD is good" (Ps. 100:5). He is good by nature and good in His dealings with us. He is kind, not cruel. This great quality of goodness might be defined as the combination of holiness and love: the goodness of God is a holy love and a loving holiness. He is good and does good. He is goodness itself.

It naturally follows that Jesus is good in this way as well. Jesus said, "I am the good shepherd" (John 10:11, 14). In a parable, He said, "I am good" (Matt. 20:15). Mere man is not good (Rom. 3:12). A young man once came to Jesus and called Him "Good Teacher." Before Jesus continued the conversation, He asked the fellow if he knew what that title implied. Jesus said, "Why do you call Me good? No one is good but One, that is, God" (Mark 10:18). Jesus did not deny being either good or God. He simply pointed out that God is good in a way that no mere man is or can be. God alone is perfectly good. Jesus wanted the young man to realize who Jesus really was. Evidently, he used the term too lightly, for he replied to Christ's next words hastily and incorrectly. He went away without following Christ. He failed to see that Jesus was not a mere "Good Teacher" but was God in the flesh.

The same is true today with those who say Jesus is only a good man or a good teacher but not God. Jesus was indeed a man and a teacher, but He is so much more. As a perfectly good man and teacher, He said He is God. If He were not God, then He would be neither a good man nor a good teacher. But Scripture teaches us that we should recognize that Jesus is perfectly good and, therefore, God. Let us not deny it, lest we become like the young man who walked away from Christ lost.

JESUS IS
the God of Grace

"God is love" (1 John 4:8, 16). Grace is the undeserved love of God. It is greater than mercy or kindness. Men may show those, but ultimately only God can show grace. The reason is that grace is forgiving love, and all sin is ultimately against God. It is truly amazing grace.

Notice how often the New Testament speaks of "the grace of our Lord Jesus Christ" (Rom. 16:20; 1 Cor. 16:23; 2 Cor. 8:9; 13:14; Gal. 6:18; Phil. 4:23; 1 Thess. 5:28; 2 Thess. 3:18; Rev. 22:21). The Bible would never dream of saying, "The grace of Michael the archangel" or "The grace of Peter the apostle." Angels and apostles cannot bestow divine grace, for they are not God. But Jesus can and does, for He is God. The apostolic benedictions call on Jesus to give grace and are thereby confessions that Jesus is the God of grace.

Many scholars argue that 2 Thessalonians 1:12 asserts the deity of Christ in the words "the grace of our God and Lord Jesus Christ." Thus God and Lord both refer to Jesus Christ. Some translations insert the article the before Lord, but it is not in the Greek text. The construction is similar to Titus 2:13 and 2 Peter 1:11, which we discussed earlier as proving the deity of Christ. The argument is well founded. On the other hand, even if Paul refers to two persons (God the Father and Jesus Christ), we are still left with the fact that he places Jesus alongside the Father, as in the frequent blessings and benedictions at the beginning and end of his epistles. Both the Father and Jesus are the source of grace. The grace of Jesus is the same as the grace of the Father. The grace of God comes only from the God of grace. If the grace of Jesus is the grace of God, what else could this mean but that Jesus is God?

JESUS IS
the God of Light

Jesus said, "I am the light of the world" (John 8:12). This is a major theme in the Gospel of John (1:4–9; 3:19; 9:5). In addition to being one of the seven "I AM" sayings in John, this speaks of His deity in a profound and wonderful way.

In 1 John 1:5, we are told that "God is light and in Him is no darkness." He is the "everlasting light" (Isa. 60:19–20). Light is as much the essence of God as His holiness or love. The light of God includes holiness, truth, and glory. When God revealed His glory in ancient Israel, it was often a bright supernatural light that the Jews called the shekinah. Yet it was only an impersonal revelation of God. Jesus, however, is the personal revelation of the light of God's glory (2 Cor. 4:4; Heb. 1:3). He came into the world of sin like a bright light shining into darkness (John 1:5). He currently dwells in unapproachable light (1 Tim. 6:16).

Jesus once showed this to three of His apostles when He was transfigured before their eyes (Matt. 17:2; Mark 9:2; Luke 9:29; 2 Peter 1:16–17). The bright shekinah glory radiated from Him. It was not a mere reflection of glory, as in angels and glorified believers (Matt. 13:43; 28:3). This was a radiance, not a reflection—a direct revelation from the source, not derived from another. It was like the sunshine rather than the moonlight. The apostles saw God's glory in Christ and knew beyond any doubt that He is the God of light (John 1:14; 2 Peter 1:16–17).

JESUS IS
the God of Glory

The one true God is "the God of glory" (Ps. 29:3; Acts 7:2). He is full of magnificent splendor and exquisite beauty. God created the universe to reveal His glory (Rom. 11:36). God is extremely jealous of His glory; He reveals it but does not give it to anyone (Isa. 42:8; 48:11). To share it would be to make the recipient another God, but that is impossible and blasphemous.

Once again, we see this Old Testament theme fulfilled in Jesus Christ. He is the glory of God and therefore the God of glory. He shared glory with the Father in eternity (John 17:5). He reveals divine glory in His person (John 1:14; 2:11). He is called "the Lord of glory" (1 Cor. 2:8; James 2:1).

Theologically, the glory of God is defined as the revelation of all that God is. It is the beauty of His being on display. That's Jesus. All that God is, Jesus is. He reveals all the attributes of God without exception. Nothing can reveal the glory of God better than God Himself. John's gospel describes how the God of glory reveals the glory of Father, Son, and Spirit (12:41; 16:14; 17:1, 5, 22, 24). The glory of God comes to us through Jesus Christ (Luke 9:32; 2 Cor. 4:4, 6; Heb. 1:3). Jesus is the glory of God and the God of glory. Second Peter 3:18 ascribes worship to Jesus in the words, "To Him be the glory both now and forever. Amen." Amen, indeed.

JESUS IS

the God of Life

There is only one "living God" (Jer. 10:10). Both God the Father and God the Son have divine life in themselves (John 5:26), and, we could add, so does the Holy Spirit. God is the source of all life (Acts 17:25). He is also immortal—He cannot die (1 Tim. 1:17).

Jesus often claimed this divine attribute for Himself: "I am the bread of life" (John 6:35); "I am the resurrection and the life" (11:25); "I am the way, the truth, and the life" (14:6). John 1:4 says, "In Him was life." He is "the Prince of life" (Acts 3:15).

Someone might ask, "If God is immortal, then how could Jesus be God, since He died?" This deserves an answer. God as God cannot die. God the Son became a mortal man to die for our sins. He was born to die. He died in His humanity, not in His deity. But since the two natures are united in His one person, Jesus could not stay dead (Acts 2:24). He allowed others to murder Him. He voluntarily laid down His life for us. He has "the power of an endless life" (Heb. 7:16). Such could only be said of God Himself.

This is illustrated in how Christ rose from the dead. The Father (Gal. 1:1) and the Spirit (Rom. 8:11) raised Christ from the dead. But John 10:17–18 also says that Jesus raised Himself. Only God has power over death (Eccl. 8:8).

Jesus said in Revelation 1:18, "I am He who lives, and was dead, and behold, I am alive forevermore.... And I have the keys of Hades and of Death." In His humanity, Christ could and did die. But not in His immortal deity. His humanity was glorified and rewarded with immortality, so He is immortal in both natures now. Perfect immortality belongs only to God; Jesus has it, and therefore He is God (1 Tim. 6:15).

JESUS

Elects Men to Salvation

God predestined everything that comes to pass (Rom. 11:36; Eph. 1:11). He planned everything in eternity, and nothing in history can thwart His eternal counsel. Salvation is included in this overall foreordination. God chose some sinners to be saved (Eph. 1:4; 2 Thess. 2:13). He made this choice solely by His own sovereign will (Eph. 1:5).

The Bible also attributes this divine work to Jesus Christ. He said, "You did not choose Me, but I chose you" (John 15:16; cf. 13:18; 15:19). The elect are chosen "in Christ"—by Christ and for Christ (Eph. 1:4). Second Timothy 1:9 says God "saved us and called us with a holy calling, not according to our works, but according to His own purpose and grace which was given to us in Christ Jesus before time began." Since only God has the prerogative to choose who will be saved, this demonstrates that Jesus is God.

Theologians call this the covenant of redemption. In eternity, the Trinity planned redemption and sealed it with a covenant. The Father chose certain sinners to be saved. He gave them to the Son. The Son volunteered to become a man and redeem them at the cross. The Spirit agreed to bring the chosen ones to Christ and apply redemption to them. In one sense, God the Father did the choosing. In another sense, Christ did the choosing. John 6 and 17 tell us about this eternal covenant. As Charles Spurgeon said, "Why should not Jesus Christ have the right to choose His own bride?" Jesus chose the elect to be His bride, a right that belongs only to God.

JESUS IS
the Son of God

The New Testament and the four Gospels in particular frequently call Jesus the "Son of God." Jesus Himself said, "I am the Son of God" (John 10:36; cf. Matt. 26:63–64; 27:43). He was the Son of God in a unique way, for He is the "only begotten" Son (John 1:14, 18; 3:16, 18; 1 John 4:9). Christians are sons of God by adoption and regeneration, but Jesus's sonship is different from ours in two important ways.

First, He was neither adopted nor regenerated but is by nature the eternal Son of God. In the incarnation Jesus had God for His Father and the virgin Mary for His mother (Luke 1:35). He received humanity from her, but He did not receive deity from the Father, for He was already God. Deity does not reproduce. Rather, the Father worked a special miracle of conception in Mary so that the eternal, preexistent Son of God would come into the world as the God-man (Gal. 4:4; 1 Tim. 1:15). Isaiah 9:6 predicted that "a Child is born…a Son is given."

Second, we do not become God or gods, but Jesus has always been God. Jesus was the Son of God before the incarnation. Theologians call this eternal generation. God the Father bore a special relation with God the Son, comparable in some respects to a human father and son. This relationship, however, has been eternal. His "goings forth are from of old, from everlasting" (Mic. 5:2). He was the Son of God within the Trinity in eternity before He was the Son of God in time (see John 3:16–17). The Jews rightly realized that the term Son of God meant deity and equality with God the Father (Mark 14:61–62; John 5:18; 10:33; 19:7). Within the Trinity, God is Father, Son, and Holy Spirit (Matt. 28:19). The Son of God is God the Son.

JESUS IS

God in the Flesh

As we have already shown, Jesus Christ existed in eternity past as God before He was born in Bethlehem. He came into the world from outside, even as He came into time from the realm of eternity (see John 1:14; 3:13; 6:62; 8:58; 17:4–5; Rom. 8:3; Gal. 4:4; Phil. 2:5–7; 1 Tim. 1:15; 1 John 3:8; 4:9–10, 14). This is the great Bible doctrine of the incarnation. Jesus was God taking on a human body of flesh, blood, and bone (Heb. 2:14; 1 John 4:2–3). "The Word was God" and "the Word became flesh" (John 1:1, 14). He is "God…manifested in the flesh" (1 Tim. 3:16).

Note the order: God became a man; man did not become a god, as Mormonism teaches. Man is not and cannot become a god, contrary to Satan's lie (Gen. 3:5; cf. Ezek. 28:9). It is heresy to say that Jesus became a god and that we can too. He is eternally God. Moreover, He did not cease being God when He became a man, contrary to Thomas J. J. Altizer's "God is dead" heresy. What's more, even when He was on earth as the God-man, He was still in heaven in His deity (John 3:13 in KJV, NKJV, and many other translations).

Whoever rejects the deity of Christ totally misses one of the basic truths of Christianity. The incarnation of Christ is a fundamental tenet of the gospel. To reject it is to reject the true gospel and be damned. God pronounces a curse on false gospels (Gal. 1:9), such as those that deny Christ's deity and incarnation. God also condemns those who say Jesus is God or a god but deny that He took on a human body and soul (1 John 4:3), as the Gnostics said. The truth is just this: God became a man. The Son of God took on a human body and soul. The Word became flesh (John 1:14). It is a deep mystery that should lead us into holy awe and profoundest worship (1 Tim. 3:16).

JESUS IS
above All Things

Several verses teach that Jesus was not just another man on earth. You could say that He was on earth but not of the earth. He Himself said He was "not of this world" (John 8:23) in contradistinction with other men. He was from outside the world and is above it in dignity and nature.

In John 3:31, John the Baptist said about Jesus, "He who comes from above is above all; he who is of the earth is earthly and speaks of the earth. He who comes from heaven is above all." Like John the Baptist, John the apostle knew that Jesus Christ "came down from heaven" (John 3:13; 6:33). Therefore, He is superior to all who are merely "of the earth." Jesus is a man but not a mere man. He came down from heaven as God and became the God-man. Obviously neither of the two Johns believed Jesus was an angel come down to become a man. In a lesser sense an angel could be said to come down from heaven, but no angel has ever taken on a human body and soul. No angel could be said to be "above all," a prerogative that belongs only to God. The Bible repeatedly says that Jesus is above all (Rom. 9:5; Eph. 1:21–22; Phil. 2:9).

First Corinthians 15:47 uses similar language in contrasting Jesus with Adam: "The first man was of the earth, made of dust; the second Man is the Lord from heaven." Adam was a mere man; Jesus shares our humanity but is so much more. He is "the Lord from heaven," a term that speaks of His deity. To deny that Jesus is God is to say He was simply another man like Adam or John the Baptist. That dismisses Scripture's plain teaching of His being "from heaven" and not "of the earth."

JESUS

Predicted the Future as Only God Can Do

God alone has perfect knowledge of the future. In fact, God says that He proves to us that He is the one true God by telling in advance what will happen in the future (Isa. 41:21–26). The heresy of open theism denies that God knows the future. Open theists worship a false god. The true God knows the future.

When God's prophecies come to pass, then people know that the Lord is God (e.g., Ezek. 6:10). God knows the future because He is omniscient and because He has foreordained all that will come to pass in history (Eph. 1:11). The biblical prophets correctly predicted the future only because God told them what would happen. Omniscience and foreordination belong to Him alone.

This is exactly what we see in Jesus. He did not predict the future as a prophet but as the omniscient God. He frequently predicted future events, some near and some distant. In some cases, God told the prophets to predict an event in the near future. When it came to pass, it validated their calling as true prophets. Failed prophecies proved others were false prophets who should be stoned (Deut. 18:22). Jesus predicted near events, such as His death and resurrection, but also others. You could say that He banked all His claims to be the Son of God on the prophecies of His death and resurrection coming to pass. If they happened, these events confirmed that He was who He said He was. In John 13:19 He said, "I tell you before it comes, that when it does come to pass, you may believe that I am He" (another I AM claim to deity).

Jesus never prefaced His prophecies with the words, "Thus says the Lord," as the prophets usually did. Instead He said, "I have told you beforehand" (Matt. 24:25). He knew the future because He is

God. Someone may object that Jesus did not know the time of the second coming (Mark 13:32). But the answer is readily at hand. He was omniscient of the future in His deity but not in His humanity. One day, all Christ's predictions of the future will come to pass. That will convince even the hardest skeptics that Jesus Christ is God.

JESUS

Was Tempted Unsuccessfully by Satan

This proof is not as obvious as the others. But upon close investigation, the truth becomes apparent. First, we know that Christ was tempted by the devil (Matt. 4:1; Mark 1:13; Luke 4:1–2; Heb. 4:15). Satan tempted Jesus in every area and threw all he had at Him but failed. Jesus at His weakest was stronger than Satan at his best. This alone implies, if not proves, His deity. But there's more to it than that.

Satan was tempting Jesus not only as a man but as God. He was challenging God to act in an ungodly way. As astounding as that may sound, it is actually typical of the nature of sin. Sin dares God. Sinners commit sin and dare God to punish them. Jesus replied to Satan, "You shall not tempt the LORD your God" (Matt. 4:7; Luke 4:12). This not only referred to Christ's refusal to test God by jumping from the top of the temple but was a rebuke to the devil for daring to test Jesus Christ as God.

First Corinthians 10:9 tells us not to tempt Christ as the Israelites did in Numbers 21. But in Numbers 21, they tempted Yahweh (Jehovah). Paul is saying that the Jews tempted Christ as God back in the wilderness, and he warns us not to imitate them. Sinners try to tempt God, but they fail because God cannot be successfully tempted to sin (James 1:13). Satan failed to tempt Christ to sin because Christ is God. Sinners also fail in their attempts to tempt Christ today, for He is still God.

JESUS

Spoke as Only God Could Speak

"No man ever spoke like this Man!" (John 7:46). Huge crowds hung on His every word (Luke 4:22). Even most non-Christians today usually admire the words of Jesus. There was something special, something otherworldly, about Christ's words. There was something supernatural about Him. What He said and how He said it caught their attention. He was no mere teacher or prophet (Matt. 7:28–29).

Only a divine Christ could have the audacity to say, "Heaven and earth will pass away, but My words will by no means pass away" (Matt. 24:35; Mark 13:31; Luke 21:33). Only God's words have eternal durability (Isa. 40:8; 1 Peter 1:23, 25).

The Old Testament prophets usually prefaced their messages with the phrase, "Thus says the Lord." This is found over four hundred times in the Bible. They dared not speak on their own authority. By contrast, it is never recorded that Jesus ever said, "Thus says the Lord." Rather, He said, "I say to you" (e.g., Matt. 5:22, 28, 32, 34, 39, 44; 18:22; John 3:5, 7, 11). Jesus was more than a prophet who spoke the word of the Lord to people. He was the Word of God Himself (John 1:1, 14; Rev. 19:13).

When men heard Jesus speak, they detected the very voice of God speaking, though in their sinful state they usually did not heed it. But God opened the hearts of some of them, as He does today, and they recognized the voice of God. If the Jews recognized the voice of God thundering at Mount Sinai, how much more can we hear the voice of God through Jesus Christ?

JESUS

Healed as Only God Could Heal

The apostles, some of the prophets, and a few others were used by God to miraculously heal sick people in Bible times. But they never claimed to heal anyone by their own power. Godly doctors today will admit the same. They give God the credit because only God can truly heal. God Himself said, "I am the LORD who heals you" (Ex. 15:26; cf. Ps. 103:3). Isaiah 35:5–6 (about God) was fulfilled in Matthew 11:3–5 (about Christ).

Jesus Christ healed thousands of people. Sometimes He did it with a touch, sometimes with mud or oil, sometimes with just a word. He healed as God and took credit for it as God. His healing proved He is the Son of God. This is evident by comparing Mark 5:19–20 with Luke 8:39, in which what God has done is equated to what Jesus has done. He healed all diseases, even those incurable by men today (Matt. 4:23; 9:35). Only God can do that.

It was not simply God healing through Jesus, as He had done with the prophets and apostles. It was the Father and the Spirit working miraculously with Christ. When Peter healed a man, the apostle confessed that it was not by his power but said, "Jesus Christ heals you" (see Acts 3:6, 16; 4:10; and especially 9:34). Every such healing was a testimony that Jesus is God.

JESUS
Performed Miracles to Prove He Is God

Jesus performed many miracles of many sorts. Some were heal-
ings. Others were miracles over the forces of nature, like walking
on water. He also cast out demons. These were all true miracles,
not sleight-of-hand magicians' tricks, let alone occult magic. They
suspended the laws of nature. Only God can work miracles.

We read in the Bible that God sometimes did miracles through
prophets, apostles, and others. It was always by God's power, not
their own. Sometimes God worked a miracle directly, without
human instrumentality. What we see in the Gospels is God working special miracles through the God-man. Christ worked miracles
by His own divine power in conjunction with the Father and the
Spirit, never as a mere man through whom God was working. He
did miracles no mere man ever did (John 15:24).

Nobody disputed that Christ's miracles were true miracles.
Some of His enemies, though, attributed them to Satan (Matt.
12:24; John 10:20). They even accused Jesus of being the devil himself (Matt. 10:25). They could not have been more wrong.

The Gospel of John intentionally records seven specific miracles
that Jesus did, and it states that these "signs" prove that Jesus is the
Son of God (John 20:30–31). The miracles performed through the
prophets and apostles only proved that they were sent from God,
not that they were God (see 2 Cor. 12:12; Heb. 2:3–4). Some of the
witnesses to Christ's miracles were amazed and as a result glorified
God (Matt. 9:8). Sometimes they wondered just who Jesus could be
to do such miracles—certainly no mere man, not even a prophet
(Mark 4:41). And sometimes a few of them grasped the meaning
of the signs. By God's grace, they realized that the miracles proved

that Jesus is God Himself in their very presence doing what only God could do.

Someone might object, "Jesus only did miracles by the Holy Spirit, as in Matthew 12:28. This was the same as the prophets and apostles who were only men." This misses the whole point. Jesus was no mere miracle-working man as they were. Jesus worked miracles as part of the Trinity. He never worked a miracle separate from the Father or the Spirit. Indeed, He frequently acknowledged their working with Him. It was like a member of a winning team giving credit to the other players on the team. This does not prove that He was a mere man but rather that He was God. What's more, we see in John's gospel that this also reveals Jesus as the second person of the Trinity.

When Jesus miraculously delivered the Gadarene man from the demons, He told him, "Go home to your friends, and tell them what great things the Lord has done for you, and how He has had compassion on you" (Mark 5:19). Of the same event, Luke says, "Tell what great things God has done for you." The man then went out and "proclaimed throughout the whole city what great things Jesus had done for him" (Luke 8:39; cf. Mark 5:20). This harmonious language in Mark and Luke is God's way of confirming that the Lord Jesus healed that man. The man obviously believed Jesus is God. So did Mark and Luke.

Take another example. Jesus walked on water (Matt. 14:25–27), which was clearly a miracle. He thus proved He is the God of whom Job had said, "He alone spreads out the heavens, and treads on the waves of the sea" (Job 9:8). Peter walked on the water only by Christ's power and permission, not his own power. When the apostles wondered who this Jesus was who could walk on the sea, He told them, "It is I," or literally in the Greek, "I am," which is the holy name of God (Matt. 14:27; cf. Ex. 3:14). When He stopped the storm, which only God can do (Pss. 89:9; 107:29), they worshiped Him and acknowledged that He was indeed the Son of God (Matt. 14:33). The miracles Christ performed, therefore, proved that He is God.

JESUS
Paid the Infinite Price for Sin

This is another proof based on Christ's special work at the cross. His miracles proved His deity, but this most important miracle of all proved it more than all His previous miracles put together. His greatest work, for which He came into the world, was the atonement. "Christ died for our sins" (1 Cor. 15:3). He was our substitute and took the wrath of God in our place. He satisfied God's holy anger and justice. This is called propitiation (Rom. 3:25; 1 John 2:2; 4:10). To understand it, we need to grasp the nature of God and the penalty for sin.

God is infinitely holy and just. Every sin against God incurs an infinite debt and incites the infinite wrath of God against the sinner. Each sin requires infinite payment, not because we are infinite but because God is infinite. We all have millions of sins to pay for, some of us more than others. Who could possibly pay such a debt? No mere man can pay, neither for himself nor for another (Ps. 49:7). The debt cannot be paid by good deeds, for those are our duty and cannot make up for our sins. Besides, we have no truly good deeds (Rom. 3:10–18). Only God can pay, for He is infinite.

This payment requires suffering and death (Rom. 6:23). Only God can pay, but God can neither suffer nor die. So, God became a man to suffer and die and thereby pay the debt to Himself. That's what we see in Jesus Christ. He is the God-man who alone can pay the infinite ransom for our redemption (Matt. 20:28; 1 Tim. 2:6). The very fact that Jesus paid what only God can pay is amazing proof is that He is indeed God.

JESUS

Raised Himself from the Dead

No man has power over death when it is his turn to die (Eccl. 8:8). God alone has power over death, for He is the Lord of life and death. He gives life; He takes it away (1 Sam. 2:6). Only God can raise the dead (Deut. 32:39).

Jesus said, "No one takes it from Me, but I lay it down of Myself. I have power to lay it down, and I have power to take it again" (John 10:18). No mere man has that kind of power. No man can stop death when it is his time to die. Jesus laid down His life voluntarily; He also raised Himself from the dead (John 2:19, 21). No mere man can do that. His resurrection proves He is the Son of God (Rom. 1:4).

Furthermore, Jesus has the unique divine authority to raise others from the dead. A few prophets and apostles did that, but only by God's power, not their own. Jesus raised several people from the dead (e.g., John 11). One day He will raise all men from the dead (John 5:21–29). Such authority is His because He has the keys of life and death (Rev. 1:18).

Jesus is neither a mere angel commissioned to take lives nor a prophet, apostle, soldier, or executioner. Those operate only at the behest of God in taking lives legally. Jesus has the authority because He is God. Only God can ransom from the dead (Isa. 25:8; Hos. 13:14 [which is quoted in 1 Cor. 15:54–55 and applied to Christ]; cf. 2 Tim. 1:10). Similarly, believing in Jesus Christ is a life-and-death matter. If we believe, we live. If we do not, we die forever.

JESUS

Defeated Satan

Some people mistakenly think that Jesus and Satan are equal in power and rank though opposite in holiness. This is a gross mistake. Actually, Satan's equal opposite is Michael (Jude 1:9; Rev. 12:7). Both are called archangels. Michael has good angels under his authority; Satan has evil angels under him. Michael defeats Satan because his angels outnumber Satan's demons and, more importantly, because God is on his side. In a one-on-one confrontation, Michael can defeat Satan only by appealing to God: "The Lord rebuke you" (Jude 1:9).

Jesus Christ is far above all angels and demons (Eph. 1:21), including Michael and Satan. Others cast out demons in Christ's name (Mark 9:38; 16:17; Luke 10:17; Acts 16:18), but Jesus cast them out in His own name (Mark 1:23–26, 32–34).

Only God has authority over Satan and the demons. Jesus defeated the demons (Col. 2:15) and Satan (Gen. 3:15; Matt. 12:22–29; John 12:31; 16:11; Heb. 2:14; 1 Peter 3:22; 1 John 3:8). He did what no mere man or angel could ever do. He defeated not one or two demons but all of them, including Satan their leader. And He did it without any help from man. How? Because He is God.

JESUS WAS

Acknowledged to Be God by the Demons

Demons may be evil, but they are not stupid. Being angels, they are far stronger than we are and know far more than we do, though they are not omniscient. They are thousands of years old and never sleep. They move behind the scenes and probably know many secrets unknown to mere humans. They seem to know at least some of our thoughts. Since the demons were once good angels in heaven, they know who God is. They once saw and worshiped God.

When Jesus ministered in Israel, the demons immediately recognized Him. They cried out, "I know who You are—the Holy One of God" (Mark 1:24). Mark 1:34 says, "They knew Him." They trembled before Jesus, knowing that as God He had the authority to cast them out and send them to hell, as He will do one day (Matt. 25:41; Rev. 20:10). Demons know God exists—and they tremble (James 2:19). They are liars, but when confronted by God in the flesh they were compelled to confess the truth. Lost sinners on judgment day will also be forced to confess that Jesus is Lord. No demon is an atheist, and no demon denies Christ's deity.

JESUS
Gave Gifts as the Ascended God

For this proof we must use the biblical principle of comparing Scripture with Scripture (1 Cor. 2:13). The inspired prophets did this (1 Peter 1:10). By seeing how an inspired New Testament writer quoted an inspired Old Testament verse, we can see more about who Jesus is.

Ephesians 4:8 describes how Christ ascended to heaven after His victorious resurrection. In consequence of this, He "gave gifts to men." This is a direct reference to Psalm 68:18, which is speaking of God Himself. Simple logic and biblical exegesis shows that Paul obviously considered Jesus to be God—and the fulfillment of this prophecy. Ephesians 4:11 then describes some of the gifts that Christ gave. But only God bestows spiritual gifts (1 Cor. 12:4–6, 11, 28). If Jesus gives what only God gives, then Jesus is God.

Psalm 47:5 also speaks of this divine ascension: "God has gone up with a shout." The pre-Christian Jews must have wondered how God could go up, since He is already everywhere and is already highly exalted. The answer is found in the New Testament. In Christ, God descended to become a man, and He later ascended in exaltation (Mark 16:19; Luke 24:51; John 3:13; 6:62; 20:17; Acts 1:2, 9; 2:33; Phil. 2:5–11; Heb. 4:14; 9:24).

Jesus, then, is God ascending and giving gifts to His people.

JESUS IS

the Only Savior

In the glorious chapters of Isaiah 40–49, the Lord proclaims that He is the one and only God. He mingles those statements with affirmations that He is the only Savior, such as, "I, even I, am the LORD, and besides Me there is no savior" (43:11; see also 43:3; 45:14, 21; 49:26; 60:16; 63:8; Jer. 14:8; Hos. 13:4; Luke 1:47; Titus 1:3). False gods cannot save. No mere man can save himself or anyone else; only God saves. The reason is that we have sinned against God, and only God can forgive us and reconcile us to Himself. He alone can rescue us from sin, death, and Satan.

Once more, we see this personified in the Lord Jesus Christ. He is repeatedly called the Savior (Luke 2:11; John 4:42; Acts 5:31; 13:23; Phil. 3:20; 2 Tim. 1:10; Titus 1:4; 2:13; 2 Peter 1:1, 11; 2:20; 3:2, 18; 1 John 4:14). His very name, Jesus, means "Yahweh saves" (Matt. 1:21). Acts 4:12 says, "Nor is there salvation in any other, for there is no other name under heaven given among men by which we must be saved."

We've just seen from various Scriptures that God is the only Savior and that Jesus is described as our Savior. Therefore, Jesus is God. He is the eternally transcendent God who became a man to save us. First Timothy 1:15 says, "Christ Jesus came into the world to save sinners." Those who believe that Jesus was only a man are lost and not saved, for they cling to a false hope that a mere man can save them. But that's not the real Jesus. The real Jesus can save us because He is God.

JESUS
Forgives Sin

Sinners deserve punishment. Unless they are forgiven, they will be sent to hell forever to suffer for their sins. The Bible tells us that only God can forgive sinners and free them from the penalty they deserve (Neh. 9:17; Isa. 43:25; Jer. 31:34).

Mark 2 records an incident in which Jesus forgave a man all his sins (v. 5). The Pharisees were incensed and thought, "Who can forgive sins but God alone?" (v. 7). They were right, but they missed the obvious fact that Jesus Christ is God. Jesus proved His claim to deity by healing the man (vv. 10–11). Luke 7 records a similar event in which they challenged His right to forgive sin. Those who deny Christ's deity are actually siding with the Pharisees. They must logically charge Christ with high presumption and blasphemy for claiming for Himself a right that belongs only to God. But then, how do they explain the miracle Jesus performed that backed up His claim?

It will not do to suggest that Jesus was simply acting as an agent of forgiveness, as if God delegated to Jesus the right to forgive sins. That would be similar to the Roman Catholic error which says that God has appointed priests as agents who can forgive sins on God's behalf. Neither idea is taught in Scripture. A preacher can proclaim God's promise and terms of forgiveness but cannot do the actual forgiving. All Christians do the same when they tell sinners the gospel (Luke 24:47). We can forgive one another in a horizontal way, as it were (Eph. 4:32), but only God can forgive sins against Himself in a vertical way.

Jesus repeatedly forgave sinners their sins (see Luke 7:48; Acts 5:31; 10:43; Eph. 1:7; Col. 2:13). Ephesians 4:32 says, "God in

Christ forgave you." The parallel in Colossians 3:13 says, "Christ forgave you." By the same standard, God alone justifies a sinner (Rom. 8:33). But so does Jesus Christ (Isa. 53:11; Acts 13:38–39; Rom. 3:24; 5:9; 1 Cor. 6:11). Jesus Christ, then, is the forgiving and justifying God.

JESUS IS
the Object of Faith

Jesus said, "Believe in God, believe also in Me" (John 14:1). He was not setting Himself up beside God as a mere man or angel, which would be outrageous presumption. Could you imagine Moses or Peter saying these words? Instead, Jesus was showing that He "was God" and "with God" (John 1:1). The Jews believed in the one true God, Yahweh. But they believed in God in only a general, almost impersonal way. Jesus called on them to believe in God by believing in Himself in a very personal way.

The Bible says repeatedly that we are saved by faith in Jesus Christ alone (e.g., Acts 20:21; Gal. 2:16, 20; 3:22, 26; Phil. 3:9). "Believe on the Lord Jesus Christ, and you will be saved" (Acts 16:31). This faith is the same as "having believed in God" in verse 34. When we truly believe in Jesus Christ as God, we are true sons of Abraham who believed God (Gen. 15:6; Gal. 3:6–9; 1 Peter 1:21).

True faith includes believing the truth about who Jesus Christ really is as both God and man. Believing that Jesus was only a man is as insufficient as believing that He was God (or a god) and not a man, as the Gnostics did. To deny His deity would mean that one trusts only in a man and not in God, but God warns us not to trust in a mere man (Pss. 118:8–9; 146:3). God says, "Cursed is the man who trusts in man.... Blessed is the man who trusts in the LORD" (Jer. 17:5, 7). The fact that the Bible calls on us to believe in Jesus Christ is proof that He is God.

JESUS

Received Worship as God

If there is one thing that God commands us, it is to worship Him (Ps. 45:11). And if there is one thing that God detests, it is idolatry—worshiping anyone or anything other than Him (e.g., Ex. 20:3–6; 22:20; 34:14–16; Deut. 11:26–28; 13:1–11; 2 Kings 17:35–36; Hos. 13:4; Rom. 1:25; 1 Cor. 10:7, 14; 1 John 5:21; Rev. 21:8; 22:15). Jesus said, "You shall worship the LORD your God, and Him only you shall serve" (Matt. 4:10).

Jesus told us to honor Him as we honor the Father: "He who does not honor the Son does not honor the Father" (John 5:23). That is not the mere honor we give to humans such as a ruler. It is worship, and we must give it to the Son in the same way we do to the Father. Only those who truly worship the Son truly worship the Father. Those who deny Christ's deity do not truly worship the Father.

It is sometimes objected that those persons merely "gave obeisance" to Jesus out of respect, not worship, perhaps like how godly Jews respected their rabbis. The Greek word is *proskuneo*, meaning "to kneel before." That word does sometimes mean only respect for a man (Matt. 18:26). But the word elsewhere certainly does mean worship of God (Matt. 4:10; John 4:23–24). Some persons knelt before Jesus merely out of respect, not realizing He was God (Mark 10:17). Others knew exactly who Jesus was and so worshiped Him as such. The epistles contain doxologies to Jesus, which are plainly divine worship, such as, "To Him be the glory both now and forever. Amen" (2 Peter 3:18; cf. 2 Tim. 4:18; Heb. 13:21; 1 Peter 4:11).

We find several examples in the Gospels of people worshiping Jesus Christ. The first were the wise men (Matt. 2:11; cf. vv. 2, 8).

Other examples include those in Matthew 8:2; 9:18; 15:25; 28:9, 17; and Mark 5:6. They did this in His very presence without a hint of rebuke (Matt. 14:33; 28:17). Had He not been God, this would have been the height of self-idolatry.

Good men (Acts 10:25–26; 14:11–18) and angels (Rev. 19:10; 22:8–9) sternly rebuked those who worshiped them. But it was appropriate for Jesus, and He received it. One day, all men will be forced to kneel before Jesus as Lord (Phil. 2:10).

To worship God also means to serve Him above all others (Matt. 4:10; Luke 4:8; both alluding to Deut. 6:13; 10:20). Christians give this ultimate service to Christ (Col. 3:24), for we realize He is God. No man can serve two masters, God and man (Matt. 6:24). We serve and worship Jesus Christ *as* God, not *instead* of God.

JESUS IS

the Uncreated Messenger of God

Hebrews 1:1–2 says that God revealed Himself gradually and in various ways before Jesus became a man. Some of the revelations were theophanies. One specific kind of theophany was the christophanies—visible manifestations of Christ before His incarnation (e.g., Josh. 5:13–15; Dan. 3:25).

One special christophany was the mysterious "Angel of the Lord." God sent many angels, but this one was markedly different. He was not merely "an angel" but "the Angel." He was neither Michael the archangel nor a second god, as some suggest. Both the Hebrew and Greek words for *angel* mean "messenger." Sometimes they refer to humans; sometimes, to angels. But in some places, the term obviously refers to a third kind of messenger. This one is God Himself, as can be seen in Genesis 31:11–13; 32:24–30; Judges 13:18–22; and Hosea 12:4–5.

This is perhaps best shown in Exodus 3. God revealed Himself to Moses in a special theophany in the burning bush. He identified Himself as "I AM WHO I AM" (v. 14). Yet Acts 7:30–35 identifies this as "an Angel of the Lord." In Genesis 16:7–13, this special Angel appeared to Hagar. She identified Him as "You-Are-the-God-Who-Sees" in verse 13. This great Messenger received worship (Ex. 3:5) and sacrifices (Judg. 13:15–23). To see Him was to see God (Judg. 13:22). On the other hand, He was somewhat different from God. He prayed to God (John 17), interceded for men (Zech. 1:12; 3:1–2), and was sent by God (John 3:17).

The mystery is solved when we turn to the New Testament. The special Angel-Messenger was Jesus Christ. He was God and yet distinct from God (John 1:1). He was God the Son with God the Father. John 1:18 says that nobody has ever seen God the Father directly, but Jesus the Son has revealed Him. Moses, Jacob, and the others did not see the Father, but they saw the Son as a christophany. The Angel of the Lord, then, was neither the Father nor the Spirit nor a mere created angel. Jesus has always been the one through whom God the Trinity reveals Himself.

This fits in with the very meaning of *messenger*—that is, someone sent with a message. Jesus frequently said He was "sent" by the Father. Hebrews 3:1 uses a similar word for *messenger* and calls Jesus the great "Apostle." He is obviously in a different category from the twelve human apostles. A man may send employees as messengers with a message but then go himself with the message. Jesus is God with the message. This fits in well with the theme in John's gospel where Jesus is "the Word" who is God (1:1, 14). One could even say that Jesus is the message itself.

As the special Angel of the Lord, He appeared only occasionally and not with a human body or soul. At the incarnation, Jesus came as a man in body and soul. It is significant that there were no more appearances of the Angel of the Lord after the resurrection. Only created angels appeared. The reason is obvious.

Lest this wonderful subject be misunderstood, it needs to be underscored again that this does not at all mean that Jesus Christ was a mere angel. Jesus created the angels (Col. 1:16); He is uncreated. Mere angels are not to be worshiped; Jesus is. Indeed, as we shall see, they worship Jesus. Much misunderstanding is avoided if we use the word *Messenger* or if we capitalize *Angel*. This one is God Himself.

JESUS IS
Worshiped by the Angels

In the context of asserting Christ's deity and showing that Jesus was not a mere angel, Hebrews 1:6 says, "When He again brings the firstborn into the world, He says: 'Let all the angels of God worship Him.'" And they did (Luke 2:13–14). They still do in heaven (Rev. 5:11–14). Isaiah 6:1–3 records the angels in heaven worshiping God (also in Rev. 4:8). John 12:39–41 says that this occurred when Isaiah saw Jesus Christ. Therefore, the angels worshiped Jesus Christ as God. They still do.

The holy angels worship God (Rev. 4:8) and refuse to be worshiped (Rev. 19:10; 22:8–9). We are forbidden to worship angels (Col. 2:18). The book of Revelation contains both the explicit worship of Jesus by angels and the explicit prohibition to worship angels. Moreover, they worship Jesus in the very holiest part of heaven itself—the last place God would ever permit it if Jesus were not God, for that would be ultimate idolatry, sacrilege, and blasphemy. Satan exalted himself as a god in heaven (Isa. 14:12–15) and was cast out with the other fallen angels.

Holy angels worshiped Jesus and were neither punished nor cast out of heaven. Indeed, God commanded it and approved of it. The angels know what they are doing, for they know beyond any doubt that Jesus Christ is God.

JESUS

Will Be Worshiped One Day by All Men

At present, very few people worship Jesus Christ as God. All true Christians—and only Christians—worship Jesus. Whoever does not worship Jesus Christ is not a true Christian. Unbelievers refuse to worship Him. Either they deny that He is God and worthy of worship, or they give only hypocritical lip service to Him.

But the day will come when everyone will worship Jesus Christ and acknowledge Him as Lord and God. Everyone who has ever lived will appear before God on judgment day (Rev. 20:12). On that day, God swears in Isaiah 45:23 that "to Me every knee shall bow, every tongue shall take an oath." This is quoted in Romans 14:11 and applied to those who appear before Christ at the judgment seat. Philippians 2:10–11 also quotes it and applies it directly to Jesus: "At the name of Jesus every knee should bow, of those in heaven, and of those on earth, and of those under the earth, and…every tongue should confess that Jesus Christ is Lord, to the glory of God the Father."

Everyone will then realize that Christ is God. They will be forced to confess it. Even the demons shall be forced to kneel. This does not at all mean that all men will be saved, let alone the demons. Demons and lost sinners will go to eternal hell (Matt. 25:41), but not before they kneel and worship Jesus Christ as Lord and God. Then they will spend eternity being punished for failing to believe in Him and worship Him as God when they were on earth. Saints and angels, however, now gladly kneel before Jesus and worship Him, and they will do so forever and ever.

JESUS

Answers Prayer

Prayer is an act of worship and, as such, can be offered only to God. We are forbidden to pray to anyone else, such as false gods and dead people (Deut. 18:10–11; Isa. 8:19). Only God answers prayer.

Jesus is involved in prayer in several ways. First, we are to pray in His name (1 John 5:14–15). That implies deity, for who could imagine that we are to pray in the name of Michael the archangel or one of the apostles or anyone else? Christ alone is our Mediator.

Christ also hears prayers, for He is God. We pray to Jesus as did Stephen (Acts 7:59), John (Rev. 22:20), Paul (1 Cor. 16:22; 2 Cor. 12:8), and the apostles (Acts 1:24–25). Jesus said, "If you ask anything in My name, I will do it" (John 14:14). He not only hears but answers prayer. He is the prayer-hearing and prayer-answering God.

Then there is Joel 2:32: "Whoever calls on the name of the LORD shall be saved." Paul quotes this in Romans 10:13 and applies it to the Lord Jesus, as Peter does in Acts 2:21. To call on the name of the Lord is to pray to and believe in Christ. Whoever calls on the name of the Lord Jesus shall be saved. Paul also alludes to Joel 2:32 in 1 Corinthians 1:2: "All who in every place call on the name of Jesus Christ our Lord."

In the Old Testament, to "call on the name of the LORD" was to pray to the one true God (Gen. 4:26; Zeph. 3:9). But if a person does not believe that Jesus is Lord and God, then he cannot pray correctly, nor will God answer his prayers.

JESUS IS

*God Who Alone Knows
the Secrets of Men's Hearts*

The Bible frequently says that God knows the secret thoughts of the hearts of all men and women (1 Chron. 28:9; Pss. 94:11; 139:1–2; Isa. 66:18; Jer. 17:10; 1 Cor. 3:20). Our thoughts are as loud to God in heaven as our words are to men on earth. God can hear the silent whimper of a broken heart as well as the unspoken hatred of an angry heart.

Notice especially 1 Kings 8:39: "You alone know the hearts of all the sons of men." God alone is omniscient, and He alone can hear what everyone is thinking. Only God knows the unexpressed evil that is within us all. Psychiatrists may guess. Parents seem to have an intuition about their children, but they too are not infallible or omniscient.

In the New Testament, we find numerous examples in which Jesus knew the secret thoughts of human hearts and minds (Matt. 9:4; Mark 2:8; Luke 6:8; 9:47; 11:17; cf. Acts 1:24; Rev. 2:23). John 2:24–25 seems to have 1 Kings 8:39 in mind when it says, "He knew all men, and had no need that anyone should testify of man, for He knew what was in man." He didn't look at a person's face and guess at his thoughts. He already knew. Nor does it ever say that Jesus knew because God told Him, which is what happened on occasion with the prophets and apostles.

First Corinthians 2:11 tells us that no man can know what is in another man's mind unless that man communicates it. But God knows without anyone telling Him. Since God alone knows, and Jesus knows, it necessarily follows that Jesus is God.

JESUS

Will Judge the Secrets of Men's Hearts

God sees everything, for He is omniscient. Ecclesiastes 12:14 says that God will one day judge the very secrets of men's hearts. He will judge their thoughts, not merely their words and works. He alone can judge, for He alone knows all.

The Bible says that God will judge the secrets of our hearts by Christ Jesus (Matt. 10:26; Mark 4:22; Luke 8:17; 12:2; Acts 10:42; 17:31; Rom. 2:16; 1 Cor. 4:5). This proves that Jesus is God. God will judge by means of Jesus Christ, for He is the God-man. It is fitting that this honor be given to Him as the obedient and victorious Messiah. For example, no one will be able to accuse the Judge of being too distant, unsympathetic, or immune to temptation. Jesus was tempted and is able to help believers and judge unbelievers. He knows the power of temptation. He knows how and why sinners give in to it, though He Himself never did.

This honor of being judge is not given to any finite creature, whether angel or human. They are not omniscient. They do not know the secrets of our hearts. Jesus does, for He is God and therefore will be the Judge.

JESUS

Will Judge the World

God is the Judge—the only Judge—because He alone is the only Creator, and it is against Him that all sins are committed. The Bible is full of statements which say that God will judge sinners on judgment day (e.g., Gen. 18:25; Pss. 50:4, 6; 96:13).

The Bible also quite clearly says that Jesus Christ is the Judge on judgment day (Matt. 16:27; 25:31–46; Luke 3:16–17; Acts 10:42; 17:31; Rom. 14:10; 1 Cor. 4:5; 2 Cor. 5:10; 2 Tim. 4:1, 8). Revelation 20:11–15 describes Jesus Christ on the throne of judgment.

Jesus said that the Father judges no one but has given the role of judge to the Son (John 5:22, 27–29). It is God the Son, therefore, not God the Father, who will be our Judge. It would be highly inappropriate for God to give this role to any created being. We will not be judged by Michael or Gabriel and certainly not by "Saint Peter at the Pearly Gates."

Those who believe in Jesus Christ, including His full deity, will be vindicated at the judgment. They have already been justified and have nothing to fear (Rom. 5:1). They will be rewarded, not punished. Unbelievers, including pseudo-Christians who deny Christ's deity, will be condemned without hope. They will realize too late that this very person they denied is in fact God their Judge.

JESUS IS

the Good Shepherd

Jesus said, "I am the good shepherd" (John 10:11, 14). He is the Shepherd of the flock of God. There is only one such Shepherd, as He Himself said in verse 16. Other New Testament writers identify Christ as "that great Shepherd of the sheep" (Heb. 13:20) and "the Shepherd and Overseer of your souls.... the Chief Shepherd" (1 Peter 2:25; 5:4).

Prophets, apostles, and pastors are only undershepherds. That is, they shepherd under the authority of the Chief Shepherd (Acts 20:28; Heb. 13:17, 20; 1 Peter 5:2–4) and are themselves sheep under Christ's pastoral rule. He is the one and only Good Shepherd. As in Psalm 23, Jesus made the people lie down in green pastures (Matt. 14:19).

The Bible teaches that God alone is the Shepherd of His flock. David sang, "The LORD is my shepherd" (Ps. 23:1). God alone is the ultimate Shepherd (Gen. 49:24; Pss. 78:52; 80:1; 100:3; Isa. 40:11; Jer. 31:10). Ezekiel 34:8–26 explicitly says that God will not leave His flock to unqualified underlings. There is a shepherding work that only God can do. Jesus did it. He is God.

The Jews who heard Jesus in John 10 knew their Hebrew Bibles well. They knew that Jesus claimed to be the Good Shepherd of Psalm 23. They knew He was claiming to be God (John 10:33). The tragic irony is that they were wolves in sheep's clothing attacking the Good Shepherd who would eventually lay down His life for the sheep. Note that Jesus explicitly said to those hypocrites, "You are not of My sheep" (John 10:26). And in saying, "I am the good shepherd," He was explicitly using the divine name I AM for Himself (Ex. 3:14). It was as if He was saying, "I am the 'I AM' God, the Good Shepherd who is the God Shepherd."

JESUS IS

the Redeemer

The Bible often says that God alone is the Redeemer (Ps. 130:7–8; Isa. 41:14; 43:14; 44:6, 22–24; 48:17; 49:7, 26; 54:5, 8; 63:9). To redeem is to buy back, to pay the price for, to ransom. Lost sinners are "sold under sin" (Rom. 7:14). To be saved, they must be bought back out of spiritual slavery. But no mere man can pay the redemption price. "None of them can by any means redeem his brother, nor give to God a ransom for him—for the redemption of their souls is costly" (Ps. 49:7–8). We have nothing to pay with either, whether money or good works. We are bankrupt. But God is infinitely rich, and He alone can pay the redemption price to buy us back. He alone is the Redeemer.

The same Bible repeatedly says that Jesus Christ is our Redeemer (Eph. 1:7; Heb. 9:12). He gave His life as a ransom to redeem us (Mark 10:45; 1 Peter 1:18–19). Jesus is "righteousness and sanctification and redemption" (1 Cor. 1:30). Since only God is the Redeemer, biblical logic demands this conclusion: Jesus Christ is God the Redeemer. To deny that is to reject the only Redeemer and forfeit redemption.

JESUS IS
the Rock

Of the many pictures and metaphors that God uses of Himself, one of the most prevalent is that of the "Rock" (Deut. 32:4, 15, 18, 30; 1 Sam. 2:2; 2 Sam. 22:2, 32; 23:3; Pss. 18:2, 31, 46; 28:1; 31:3; 42:9; 71:3; 89:26). He is *the Rock*, not merely *a* rock. He is more solid and dependable than the Rock of Gibraltar.

The New Testament uses this same imagery for Jesus Christ: "That Rock was Christ" (1 Cor. 10:4; cf. Matt. 21:42; Rom. 9:32–33; Eph. 2:20; 1 Peter 2:4–8). Isaiah 28:16 is referred to several times in the New Testament in reference to Christ the foundation stone. Jesus Himself referred to the rock imagery of Psalm 118:22 and applied it to Himself. To deny Jesus is to fall on this Rock and have it crush you (Luke 20:18). Thus, to deny that Jesus is the divine Rock is to fatally set ourselves up for destruction. He is the Rock of shelter for believers and a rock of destruction for unbelievers. This could only be said of God.

Isaiah 8:14 also speaks of Jehovah being a "stone of stumbling and a rock of offense." Note that this verse is quoted in Romans 9:33 and 1 Peter 2:6, 8 and applied to Jesus. This is but one instance in which the Holy Spirit infallibly interpreted such Old Testament verses about Jehovah and applied them to Jesus Christ, the Rock.

JESUS IS
the Crucified God

Zechariah 12:10 is one of several Old Testament prophecies of the crucifixion. It says, "They will look on Me whom they pierced." The "Me" is none other than Jehovah God Himself (vv. 1, 4). The piercing is the same as predicted in Psalm 22:16: "They pierced My hands and My feet." The Jews in Old Testament times were mystified as to how these prophecies would be fulfilled, for they did not practice crucifixion. Further, how could God Himself, who has no body, be pierced?

The answer is in the fulfillment recorded in all four Gospels. John 19:37 and Revelation 1:7 explicitly apply Zechariah 12:10 to Jesus. Matthew 27:35 quotes Psalm 22:18 and thereby indicates that it was fulfilled in the crucifixion of Christ. Luke 24:39 implies it as well.

But note also that Zechariah 12:10 says both "Me" and "Him." This is God (vv. 1, 4) but specifically a "son." That's God the Son, Jesus Christ. Indeed, if you look closely, the whole Trinity is in this verse. The Father pours out the Spirit on those who then behold the Son who is crucified. In sum, Jesus is the crucified God of Zechariah 12:10.

JESUS IS

Lord over the Angels

Many of those who reject the deity of Christ say that He was only an angel. Some suggest He was Michael the archangel. But this goes squarely against the clear and repeated teaching of Scripture. Hebrews 1:5–14 makes several explicit statements that Jesus is not and never has been an angel, such as, "To which of the angels did [God] ever say.... But to the Son He says" (vv. 5, 8). Jesus is "better than the angels" (v. 4). The book of Hebrews says that Christ is the superlative one because He is better than angels, Moses, Joshua, Levi, and others. He is not the best angel. He is not an angel at all. Hebrews 1 clearly states that He is God.

Hebrews 2:7–16 continues the point. Jesus is God who became a man to save men. He did not become an angel to save angels. Good angels need no salvation, and there is no salvation for the bad angels. He died for men, not angels. Nor was Jesus an angel who became a man. He is the God-man, not the angel-man.

Angels are created beings, but Jesus created the angels and is Himself uncreated (Col. 1:16). The angels belong to Jesus (Matt. 13:41; 16:27; 24:31; 2 Thess. 1:7). Mark 13:32 explicitly differentiates between Jesus and the angels. Michael, not Jesus, is the counterpart to Satan (Jude 1:9; Rev. 12:7). Jesus is superior to both Satan and Michael, for Jesus is "far above" all angels, good or bad (Eph. 1:21).

Moreover, the holy angels worship God alone (Ps. 148:2). However, they also worship Jesus. "When He again brings the firstborn into the world, He says: 'Let all the angels of God worship Him'" (Heb. 1:6, quoting Ps. 97:7; cf. Luke 2:13). The angels certainly did not worship another angel. Angels are not to be worshiped (Col. 2:18), and they vehemently refuse to be worshiped (Rev. 19:10; 22:8–9). Jesus willingly accepted the worship of the holy angels. If He were not God but only an angel, then He would have been an evil angel to accept worship that belongs only to God. But the fact that He is God is the logical conclusion and a warning to those today who contend wrongly that Jesus was only an angel. They thereby side with the evil angels in refusing to worship Jesus as God rather than joining the holy angels in worshiping Christ.

JESUS IS
the Lord of Baptism

The holy ordinance of baptism is an implicit assertion of the deity of Christ. In Matthew 28:19, Jesus commanded, "Baptizing them in the name of the Father and of the Son and of the Holy Spirit." This is the Trinity, the one true God who exists eternally in three persons. The three members share the same divine name in which baptism is to be performed. We find examples of baptism in the name of Jesus in Acts 2:38; 8:16; 10:48; and 19:5. To be baptized in Christ's name is to be baptized in the name of the Trinity. The Son is as much God as the Father and the Holy Spirit are.

Paul explicitly says that Christian baptism is not performed in the name of any mere man, even an apostle such as himself (1 Cor. 1:12–17). And baptism is certainly not done in the name of an angel. Imagine how ridiculous, if not blasphemous, it would be to baptize someone "in the name of Gabriel the angel" or "in the name of Mary the mother of Jesus." Even Roman Catholics, who practically deify Mary, would never dream of doing that. Baptism symbolizes that we are saved by God alone.

Since baptism is performed in the name of the Trinity as well as in the name of Jesus Christ, the obvious conclusion is that Jesus Christ is a member of the holy Trinity and is therefore God.

JESUS IS

the Husband of God's Wife

This proof is not well known but is arrived at by comparing Scripture with Scripture. The Bible occasionally uses the metaphor of God being a husband with a wife (Isa. 54:5; 62:5; Jer. 3:14; Hos. 2:16, 19). His wife is His people who belong to Him in a special way of covenantal love and have an intimate relationship with Him comparable to that of a husband and wife. God forbids polygamy (several wives) and polyandry (several husbands) as well as adultery. Lamech, Jacob, David, Solomon, and others were wrong to marry several wives simultaneously. But God has only one wife. He is not a polygamist, as the Mormons teach. His wife has only one husband.

The New Testament continues to employ the same metaphor. In keeping with the uniform New Testament pattern, the Old Testament is fulfilled in Jesus Christ. He is frequently described as a husband (Matt. 9:15; 22:2–14; 25:1–13; Mark 2:19–20; Luke 5:34–35; 12:35–40). John the Baptist was the "best man," as it were (John 3:29). Christ's bride is the church (2 Cor. 11:2; Eph. 5:25–32; Rev. 19:7, 9; 21:2, 9).

Putting all these verses together, we see that Jesus is God. His wife consists of believers in both the Old and New Testament. They are *the bride*, not separate brides, as some dispensationalists imply. God has only one bride, and she has only one husband. To deny that Jesus is God is to say that God allows His wife to have another husband. But God honors the holy ordinance of marriage, and so does Christ. The mystery is that Christ is the divine husband of the wife of God.

JESUS

Has Witnesses That He Is God

"'You are My witnesses,' says the LORD" (Isa. 43:10; 44:8). This is in the middle of that great section of Isaiah 40 to 49 in which the Lord (Jehovah) boldly asserts His unique deity in several attributes. His people are witnesses that the Lord is God.

This is alluded to in Acts 1:8 when Jesus said to the apostles, "You shall be witnesses to Me" (cf. 22:15). They were commissioned to testify that Jesus is the divine Messiah and Savior. The witnesses of Jehovah in the Old Testament are basically the same as the witnesses of Jesus in the New Testament. Both testify that the Lord alone is God, that Jesus is Jehovah.

The so-called Jehovah's Witnesses deny this. They thereby show they are not the true witnesses of Jehovah and Jesus. They bear false witness against Jehovah. The believing Jews in Isaiah's day and the Christians in Christ's day through to the present have been the true witnesses of Jehovah, for they believed Jesus was Jehovah.

JESUS

*Commissioned the Apostles
and Prophets*

In addition to the apostles sent out in Acts 1:8, Jesus commissioned Paul to be a special apostle equal in authority to them. Notice the words of Galatians 1:1 very carefully: "Paul, an apostle (not from men nor through man, but through Jesus Christ and God the Father who raised Him from the dead)." Paul explicitly says he was not commissioned by a mere man but by Jesus Christ. Obviously, Paul did not consider Jesus to be a mere man. He puts Him alongside God the Father, as Jesus Himself did regularly in the Gospel of John and the baptismal formula of Matthew 28:19.

This applies to inspired prophets as well as apostles. Jesus said, "I send you prophets, wise men, and scribes" (Matt. 23:34). The parallel in Luke 11:49 says, "I will send them prophets and apostles." Ephesians 4:8–11 speaks of Christ bestowing spiritual gifts following His ascension: "And He Himself gave some to be apostles, some prophets, some evangelists, and some pastors and teachers" (v. 11). First Corinthians 12:7–11, 28 states that God (specifically the Holy Spirit) gives the gifts of apostleship and prophecy. God sent Isaiah as a prophet (Isa. 6:8–9). John 12:41 says Isaiah saw Jesus sending him, and by inference we can say that Jesus sent the rest of the Old Testament prophets. Revelation 22:6 identifies God as "the Lord God of the holy prophets." The clear teaching of these verses is that God alone sends true prophets. Because Jesus sends them, He is therefore God.

JESUS

Was Seen by Isaiah as God on the Throne

The Gospel of John presents the deity of Jesus Christ in a variety of ways. In John 12:39–41, John tells us that Isaiah the prophet saw Jesus on the throne in heaven. This is a reference to Isaiah 6:1–9, the only instance in Isaiah's prophecy in which he saw God on the throne. Note that he specifically calls Him "LORD" (v. 3)—that is, Jehovah (Yahweh).

The book of Isaiah is the fullest prophecy of the person and work of the coming Messiah. The gospel according to Isaiah foretold Christ's virgin birth (7:14), sufferings, and death (53:1–12). He also said that this Messiah would be God (9:6).

Isaiah saw that this would be the same One on the throne of Isaiah 6. If he could somehow have been transported forward to the time of Jesus, he would have testified that Jesus Christ was the very One he had seen hundreds of years earlier in his inspired visions. Isaiah foresaw Jesus not only on the cross but on the throne. Those who deny Christ's deity are at odds with Isaiah the inspired eyewitness.

JESUS

Gives Grace and Peace with the Father

Most of the New Testament epistles begin or end with a benediction that is basically this: "Grace to you and peace from God our Father and the Lord Jesus Christ" (Rom. 1:7; 1 Cor. 1:3; 2 Cor. 1:2; 13:14; Eph. 1:2; 6:23; Phil. 1:2; Col. 1:2; 1 Thess. 1:1; 2 Thess. 1:2; 1 Tim. 1:2; 2 Tim. 1:2; Titus 1:4; Philem. 1:3; 2 John 1:3). Revelation 1:4–5 includes all three members of the Trinity in the benedictory blessing.

To place a mere creature next to God the Father in such blessings would be idolatry and presumption of the highest order. Even the apostles did not include themselves in the blessings—they gave their greetings separately. They prayed for the bestowal of blessing but could not give it. Only God can give grace and peace.

John the apostle taught this truth in another way. He showed that Jesus Christ bestowed both grace (John 1:16) and peace (14:27). This was in keeping with his theme that Jesus is God and the means by which God gives salvation and all other blessings (cf. Eph. 1:3). To deny Christ's deity is to forfeit those blessings, including saving grace and peace.

JESUS IS
the Lord of the Law

In Matthew 5:17–19, Jesus said that He did not come to abolish the law but to fulfill it. He fulfilled the law even as He fulfilled the prophecies of the Messiah. He obeyed the moral laws perfectly and did not annul any of them. The Bible describes many ceremonial laws that were basically symbolic in nature (Col. 2:16–17) and were meant only for the Jews until Messiah came. They were prophetic in nature and have been fulfilled and abolished.

When Jesus came as Messiah, He kept all the ceremonial laws. He fulfilled their prophetic significance and thereby set them aside as no longer necessary or binding (Eph. 2:15; Col. 2:16–17; Heb. 7:12; 9:9–10). For example, He abolished the ceremonial laws concerning clean and unclean foods (Acts 10:9–16; Rom. 14:17; Col. 2:16–17; Heb. 9:9–10). He was the perfect and final sacrifice for sin, so He fulfilled the typological significance of the Old Testament sacrifices and abolished them (see Heb. 7–10).

Christ replaced the intricate old covenant ceremonial laws with two simple ceremonies: baptism and the Lord's Supper (Matt. 26:26–29; 28:19; Mark 14:22–25; 16:16; Luke 22:17–20; 1 Cor. 11:23–25).

Then consider the institution of the Sabbath, one of the Ten Commandments (Ex. 20:8–11). God called it "My holy day" (Isa. 58:13), for God alone ordained the Sabbath (Gen. 2:3). Jesus said that He was the Lord of the Sabbath (Matt. 12:8; Mark 2:28; Luke 6:5). No mere man could claim that. Jesus changed the Sabbath day from Saturday to Sunday in memory of His resurrection, again, something only God could dare to do.

The point is this: only God has the authority to change the law in any respect. Jesus did so because He is God. Indeed, the law of God is the law of Christ (1 Cor. 9:21; Gal. 6:2). Jesus is the Lord of the law, the Lawgiver Himself. James 4:12 says, "There is one Lawgiver." Moses only delivered the law. Jesus gave it and has the right to change it because He is God.

JESUS IS

to Be Followed as God

Elijah confronted the apostate Israelites who heeded the false prophets of Baal. He boldly thundered, "If the LORD is God, follow Him; but if Baal, follow him" (1 Kings 18:21). The logic is perfect. We are to follow the one true God alone, not false gods. If the Lord is God, we must follow Him. We creatures must follow our Creator. To follow means giving ultimate allegiance of faith, love, obedience, and worship.

The prophets said, "Follow God." Jesus said, "Follow Me" (Matt. 4:19; 8:22; 9:9; 16:24; 19:21; Mark 1:17; 2:14; 8:34; 10:21; Luke 5:27; 9:23, 59; 18:22; John 1:43; 12:26; 21:19, 22). This was neither a suggestion nor merely good advice. It was a command that only God could give. Jesus did not say, "Follow My example," as if He were a mere man. We are to follow His example in some things, but more than that, we are to follow Him. He calls on us to follow Himself in the same way that Elijah called on the Israelites to follow the Lord.

Jesus said that His sheep follow Him (John 10:3–5, 27). They follow Him everywhere, even to heaven (Rev. 14:4). To follow Christ means to follow Him unreservedly, being ready to die for Him with unquestioned allegiance. Such could be given only to God. To deny Christ's deity is not to follow Him. As in Elijah's day, to refuse to follow Jesus as God is to follow a false god, even Satan (2 Cor. 4:4). There is no other option—you either follow Jesus or you follow Satan.

JESUS IS

*the Lord Our Righteousness
and Sanctification*

God is righteousness itself. He is ultimate holiness and justice. He is "THE LORD OUR RIGHTEOUSNESS" (Jer. 23:6; 33:16). The Lord alone possesses righteousness and strength (Isa. 45:24).

Jesus is also called "the Holy One" and "the Just One" (Acts 3:14; 7:52; 22:14). The righteousness of God comes to us only in Jesus Christ (Rom. 3:21–22; 2 Cor. 5:21; Phil. 3:9). When God justifies us by faith, He puts the very righteousness of Christ to our account. Jesus was a righteous man (Luke 23:47), but He was far more—He was righteousness itself (1 Cor. 1:30).

Similarly, Exodus 31:13 and Leviticus 20:8 say, "I am the LORD who sanctifies you." In the New Testament, it is Jesus who sanctifies His people (Eph. 5:25–26; Titus 2:13–14; Heb. 13:12). There is only one sanctifier, not two. Jesus did not take over this role from God; He actually is the God who sanctifies. Thus, Jesus is our legal righteousness in justification and produces holiness in us by sanctification. He is "righteousness and sanctification" (1 Cor. 1:30). That could never be said of a mere man or even a holy angel. It could only be said about one who is God.

JESUS IS
the Sovereign of the Kingdom of God

We have already shown that the Bible asserts the deity of Christ by referring to Him as King and the King of kings. This is also shown in His role as the sovereign ruler of the kingdom of God. In all four Gospels, especially Matthew, Jesus proclaimed the arrival of the kingdom of God (also called the kingdom of heaven). He invited sinners to enter it by repentance and faith in Him (Mark 1:15). Matthew combined two themes: Jesus is the King, and He proclaimed the kingdom of God. This is a clear assertion that Jesus rules the kingdom of God, a role that can belong to God alone.

Ephesians 5:5 calls it "the kingdom of Christ and God." Revelation 11:15 says, "The kingdoms of this world have become the kingdoms of our Lord and of His Christ." These are not two different kingdoms and two kings. Rather, it is parallel to what Jesus said in John 10:16: "One flock and one shepherd."

The kingdom of God obviously has only one king. If Jesus were not God, then the Jews were right to execute Him as a usurper to God's throne and an evil revolutionary against Him. But the glory is that Jesus Christ was—and still is—the ruler of the kingdom of God by eternal divine right. King Jesus is God.

JESUS IS
the Head of the Church

The Bible uses this metaphor several times. Jesus bears a relation to His people as a head to a body (Eph. 1:22; 4:15; 5:23; Col. 1:18). He is the Head in the sense that He has full authority over us (Eph. 5:24).

First Corinthians 1:10–17 says that no mere man can have that kind of authority. That applies to popes, apostles, prophets, and pastors. The church is a body with only one Head. Likewise, Christ has only one body, not several. He occupies this special role as God.

A civil state has a head, be he king, pharaoh, caesar, or president. The church is not only a body but a kingdom (Matt. 16:18–19). It has a Head who is King. Only God is the Head and King. Jesus is described as having both roles; therefore, we can confidently affirm that Jesus is God.

Hebrews 3:2–6 uses a similar argument. God appointed Moses to be a steward over the people of God, who are likened to a house. But Jesus is superior to Moses, for He is the builder and owner of the house, not a mere steward. Verse 4 is especially poignant: "He who built all things is God." Jesus said, "I will build My church" (Matt. 16:18). Jesus built the church as the building of God, for He is the Head of the church.

JESUS IS

the Namesake of the Church

No church can rightly be named after a mere man (1 Cor. 1:10–17). Churches that are named after their founder, such as Lutherans, Mennonites, or Wesleyans, should take note. The name of a church indicates ownership. The church belongs to God. It is "the church of God" (Acts 20:28; 1 Cor. 10:32) and "the church of the living God" (1 Tim. 3:15).

Local churches are "the churches of Christ" (Rom. 16:16). Jesus called it "My church" (Matt. 16:18). It is named for its owner. Does this not indicate that Jesus is God?

The New Testament does not give specific names to individual local churches. They are simply described in terms of location, like "the church of God which is at Corinth" (1 Cor. 1:2). Later they chose specific names to differentiate themselves from other churches in the same city and from false churches. Over time, names sometimes emphasized certain distinctive doctrines or practices, like Baptist or Presbyterian. Be that as it may, both the local and universal church belong to the Lord Jesus Christ, not to any mere man.

JESUS IS
Lord of the Temple

The temple is frequently referred to in the Bible as "the temple of the Lord" and "the temple of God." Malachi 3:1 says, "The Lord…will suddenly come to His temple." It was the true temple, not like the temples of false gods. God dwelt in the temple in a special way. He showed His glory and received worship and sacrifices. It was a holy place. But, of course, God Himself was greater than the temple and could not be confined to it (2 Chron. 6:18). No mere man is greater than the temple.

Jesus shocked people by saying that He was greater than the temple (Matt. 12:6). He cleansed it as only God had the right to do, even referring to it as "My house" (Matt. 21:13; Mark 11:17; Luke 19:46; cf. John 2:13–16). It would have been sacrilege and blasphemy for anyone else to do that.

When Jesus died, the veil of the temple was torn in two. This signified that men would now have direct access to God through Him (Eph. 2:18; Heb. 10:20). The temple, like many Old Testament ceremonies, was fulfilled and abolished. The true temple had come—Jesus Christ Himself (John 2:19–21). By extension, His body of believers is His temple (1 Cor. 3:16–17; 6:19; 2 Cor. 6:16; Eph. 2:21–22). Whoever sets himself up as Lord in God's temple sets himself up as God. This is the Antichrist (2 Thess. 2:3–4). If Jesus were not truly God, claiming such a thing falsely would make Him the Antichrist. But He is rightly enthroned in the temple of Christians, for He is God.

When Solomon dedicated the temple to replace the tabernacle, he prayed, "But will God indeed dwell on the earth? Behold, heaven and the heaven of heavens cannot contain You. How much less this temple which I have built!" (1 Kings 8:27). But God did later dwell on the earth when He became a man. John 1:14 says, "The Word became flesh and dwelt among us, and we beheld His glory." The word dwelt in the original Greek literally means "tabernacled." God dwelt on the earth in the person of Jesus Christ and revealed His glory there. Also, there is no physical temple in heaven, for the true and ultimate temple is the Lord God Almighty and Jesus (Rev. 21:22). Jesus is both the Lord of the temple and the temple of the Lord.

JESUS

Has the Name of God

In the Old Testament, "the name" was a reference to God (Ex. 3:13–15; 20:7; Lev. 24:11, 16). "Blessed be the name of the LORD" (Job 1:21) means "blessed be the Lord." God is holy, and His name is holy. It stands for who and what God is. To bless or curse His name is to bless or curse God. The third commandment warns us about taking the name of the Lord in vain (Ex. 20:7).

When we come to the New Testament we see the same principle applied to Jesus Christ. He is "the name" (cf. Acts 5:41; 9:21; 3 John 1:7). He has "the name which is above every name" (Phil. 2:9; cf. Eph. 1:21). Acts 4:12 says there is salvation in no other name than the name of Jesus. Hence, we are to pray, meet, and cast out demons in His name. Matthew 28:19 says we are to baptize in "the name of the Father and of the Son and of the Holy Spirit."

The Old Testament often uses the phrase "in the name of the LORD" (e.g., Ps. 118:26). This is clarified in the New Testament phrase "in the name of Jesus Christ" (Acts 2:38; 3:6; cf. 4:10, 18, 30; 5:40; 8:12, 16; 9:14–16, 27; 10:43, 48; 15:26; 16:18; 19:5, 13, 17; 21:13; 22:16; 26:9; 1 Cor. 5:4; 2 Thess. 3:6). There is no precedent for doing anything of such importance in the name of a mere man, even an apostle (cf. 1 Cor. 1:13–15) or an angel.

This, of course, is not confined to the specific pronunciation of the name Jesus, whether in Hebrew as Yeshua or Greek as Iesous. It refers to His person. His name speaks of His deity, for it means "Jehovah saves" (cf. Matt. 1:21). His lesser-known personal name, Immanuel, also verifies His deity, for it means "God with us" (Matt. 1:23, quoting Isa. 7:14).

JESUS IS

the Source and Object of the Gospel

The gospel is called "the gospel of God" (Rom. 1:1; 15:16; 2 Cor. 11:7)—it is both from God and about God. It is also called "the gospel of Christ" (Rom. 15:19; 2 Cor. 9:13; 10:14; 1 Thess. 3:2)—it is from Christ and about Christ. Jesus Himself preached the gospel of God when He preached about Himself.

There is only one true gospel (Gal. 1:6–9). It is the good news about who Jesus Christ really is: that He was God in the flesh, God become a man to die for our sins (1 Cor. 15:1–4). It all falls apart if Jesus is not God. Indeed, it would be just another false gospel with false hope, for no mere man can truly save us. Such is the case with the false gospels of those who deny the deity of Christ. They are under God's curse (Gal. 1:9).

JESUS IS
the Living One

God not only exists, He lives. Unlike us, God has life in Himself. We live only because God gives us life (Acts 17:25). But no one gives life to God. He is the source of all life.

The Bible often calls God "the living God" (Josh. 3:10; Pss. 42:2; 84:2; Hos. 1:10; Matt. 16:16; 26:63; Acts 14:15; Rom. 9:26; 2 Cor. 3:3; 6:16; 1 Tim. 3:15; 4:10; Heb. 3:12; 9:14; 10:31). False gods are dead. God is immortal and cannot die. He is the living One par excellence.

In Revelation 1:18, Jesus said, "I am the Living One" (NIV). He said more than simply, "I am alive." He was saying that He is the Living One, the source of life, who cannot ultimately die. When Jesus became a man to die for our sins, He died in His humanity, not His deity. But because He is both God and man, it was not possible for Him to stay dead (Acts 2:24).

In using "the Living One" of Himself, Jesus declared that He is the living God and the source of all life.

JESUS IS
the God of Isaiah 40

Shortly before Jesus began His ministry, John the Baptist announced that the Messiah was coming. Matthew 3:3 quotes from Isaiah 40:3 and applies it to John's work as the herald who prepared the way for the Lord. John later identified Jesus as the Messiah and directed people to follow Him. His work done, John the Baptist began to fade away.

The key is in what John quoted: "The voice of one crying in the wilderness: 'Prepare the way of the LORD; make His paths straight'" (Matt. 3:3; Mark 1:3; Luke 3:4; cf. Luke 1:76; John 1:23; Acts 19:4). When you look at Isaiah 40:3, it is plainly obvious that "the LORD" there is none other than Yahweh. The whole chapter is about Him who is God (see vv. 1, 3, 8, 9, 18, 27, 28, 31). He is "the Lord GOD" (v. 10) and "the Creator" (v. 28). This is the One whose path would be prepared by John the Baptist.

Isaiah 40:11 also alludes to God being a shepherd. Jesus referred to this in John 10:11: "I am the good shepherd." Isaiah 40, then, speaks of God and is distinctly applied to Jesus Christ in the New Testament. This is no coincidence. In light of such clear teaching, to deny that Jesus is the Jehovah of Isaiah 40 is to say that John the Baptist, the four Gospel writers, and Jesus Himself were all wrong. But they were not.

JESUS IS

the God of Malachi 3 and 4

Malachi was sent to rebuke Israel for turning away from God. He foretold future blessings when the Messiah would come. But before then, he said God would send another prophet like Elijah to prepare the way of Messiah (Mal. 3:1; 4:5). This is the same prophecy as Isaiah 40:3.

Jesus said that John the Baptist was the forerunner messenger predicted in Malachi (Matt. 11:10–14; cf. 17:10–13; Mark 1:2–3). Gabriel the angel also said so (Luke 1:17). John was not a resurrected Elijah (John 1:21) but rather a bold prophet like him. Both were fearless and rugged, rebuking Israel and calling her back to God. In fact, Jesus said John was the greatest man who ever lived (Matt. 11:11). Why? Among other things, he had the privilege of introducing the Messiah to Israel. He was the "best man" at the Messiah's wedding, as it were (John 3:29), and as such prepared the way for Him (v. 28).

Now the point is that Malachi's prophecy specifically says that this great forerunner would "prepare the way before Me," who is "the Lord, whom you seek" (3:1). John prepared the way for the Lord Jesus Christ. Plain biblical exegesis and logic indisputably show that the promised Lord of Malachi is the Lord Jesus of Matthew.

At first John the Baptist did not realize Jesus was anyone more than his cousin (John 1:31). Then God opened his eyes and he recognized Jesus as the Messiah promised by Isaiah and Malachi. Since he knew that he was the predicted forerunner, he certainly realized that Jesus was the Lord Himself. Thus, John humbly admitted that he was not worthy to untie Christ's sandals and needed baptism from Him (Matt. 3:11, 14).

John the Baptist would thunder damnation at those today who deny the deity of Jesus Christ.

JESUS

Will Return as God

The Old Testament contains many dire warnings that the Lord God will personally come to earth in worldwide judgment (e.g., Ps. 96:13; Isa. 40:10; 66:15). Some were fulfilled indirectly and in part when He providentially punished Israel, Egypt, Assyria, or Babylon. Others obviously have not happened yet.

Jesus fulfilled the prophecies of God personally by coming to earth in salvation. His second coming will fulfill the prophecies of God coming to earth in judgment. For example, Jude 1:14–15 says, "The Lord comes with ten thousands of His saints, to execute judgment on all." Other such examples show how the New Testament writers used Old Testament wording that predicted the coming of God in judgment and applied them to the second coming of Jesus Christ.

It is particularly interesting that the New Testament does not specifically predict the coming of God but of Jesus Christ. In the authors' minds, they are the same event. They believed that Jesus Christ is God. This is yet another example of how inspired New Testament writers applied Old Testament verses about God to Jesus Christ. They did it with reference to both His first and second comings.

When Christ comes again, all who have denied that He is God will have an extremely rude awakening. They will be utterly terrified (Rev. 6:15–17). For as both Testaments predict, He will come in violent vengeance to punish all unbelieving sinners (2 Thess. 1:7–9). Those who preach a false gospel that denies Christ's deity will suffer a special condemnation. The wrath of Jesus Christ is the wrath of God.

JESUS IS
Our Ultimate Teacher

God has sent and gifted many persons to be spiritual teachers. Some were prophets; others were apostles. But they were all just humans, nothing more. We thank God for them, but we dare not deify them (cf. 1 Cor. 3:5–7). Some were directly inspired to write Scripture and were thereby infallible on those occasions (2 Tim. 3:16–17; 2 Peter 1:20–21). No teacher since then is either inspired or infallible, and certainly none are divine, though many false teachers have claimed to be all three.

Jesus said several things that, put together, show He was God the one great Teacher above all others. First, many Jews realized that Jesus was a teacher, a rabbi (John 1:38). Nicodemus, one of the most respected rabbis in Israel at that time (John 3:10), admitted that Jesus was "a teacher come from God" (John 3:2). A rich young ruler called Jesus "Good Teacher," but he failed to see that Jesus was more than a human good teacher (Mark 10:17–22).

Later, Jesus warned us against calling or being called teacher, for in the ultimate sense, "One is your Teacher, the Christ" (Matt. 23:8–10). Then in John 13:13, He said, "You call Me Teacher and Lord, and you say well, for so I am." He is the greatest Teacher, for He is Lord—that is, God. Note that this may be yet another I AM saying of Christ in John's gospel.

When we take all these verses together, the conclusion is inescapable: Jesus Christ is the Lord God, our ultimate Teacher unlike any mere rabbi or preacher the world has ever known.

JESUS IS
Our Only Master

This proof is not as obvious as some others, for it is based on a specific Greek word used in the original New Testament. It is the word *despotes*, meaning "master, lord, owner." We get the English word despot from it. A *despot* has absolute authority. The Greek New Testament uses this word to describe God in Luke 2:29; Acts 4:24; and Revelation 6:10 as well as several times in the Greek translation of the Hebrew Old Testament.

Jude 1:4 applies the word to Jesus Christ. He is "our only Master and Lord, Jesus Christ" (NASB). Here the words *Master* and *Lord* are used synonymously and both refer to Jesus. Some manuscripts and translations (such as the NKJV) add "God" after the first term. Jude's letter is based on 2 Peter 2, often using the exact same words. The parallel to Jude 1:4 is 2 Peter 2:1, "even denying the Lord [*Despotes*] who bought them." Jesus bought us by means of His own precious blood. Jude (v. 4 NASB) says Jesus is "our only Master," while elsewhere the Bible says God is our only Master. There can be only one such Master (cf. Matt. 6:24).

Despotes is used several other places to refer to slave owners (1 Tim. 6:1–2; Titus 2:9; 1 Peter 2:18). A Christian is a slave of God (Titus 1:1), a slave of Jesus Christ (Rom. 1:1; 1 Cor. 7:22; Gal. 1:10; Col. 4:12; 2 Peter 1:1; Jude 1:1), a "bondservant of God and of the Lord Jesus Christ" (James 1:1). Since there is only one Master of Christians, this shows that Jesus Christ is God. He is our absolute Master, and we are glad He is.

JESUS IS
the King of the Jews

One of the main themes of the Gospel of Matthew is that Jesus Christ is the King of the Jews. In chapter 1, Matthew traces His lineage through Joseph, His adoptive father, back to David and Abraham. Jesus was descended from David and would have been the rightful heir to the throne. Though not literally crowned as such, He was in this sense the King of the Jews (see, e.g., Matt. 2:2; 27:11; John 1:49; 12:13–15; 18:36–37; 19:19).

Matthew took this to a higher spiritual level. Jesus did not bring in a physical or political kingdom but rather the spiritual kingdom of God. The citizens of that kingdom are Jews and Gentiles who believe in Jesus.

God alone is the King of the Jews and Israel—even of the world—far more than David ever was (1 Sam. 8:7; Pss. 24:7–10; 90:1; 95:3; 96:10; 97:1; 99:1; Isa. 43:15). There are not two kings of the Jews. The Romans installed Herod as a puppet king over Israel. He was deadly jealous when he heard the wise men speak of a newborn "King of the Jews" (Matt. 2:2). He thought he was the true king of the Jews. He wasn't.

God is also jealous for His kingship over the Jews. He was grieved when Israel wanted a mere human king (1 Sam. 8). But He is pleased with Jesus being the King of the Jews, for as we have repeatedly seen, Jesus is God come down to earth in human form to be King and Savior.

JESUS IS

the Perfect and Only Mediator

Man needs a mediator with God because of sin. He needs just the right person to accomplish reconciliation between God and man. Jesus is that Mediator (1 Tim. 2:5). The true Mediator had to be both God and man to sympathize with both. It would be something like Timothy, half-Greek and half-Jew. Timothy could sympathize with both Jews and Greeks and could possibly be their mediator in a dispute (Acts 16:1). Jesus feels for man because He is a man (Heb. 4:15). He feels for God, if we can put it like that, because He is God (Heb. 1).

It would be totally foreign to biblical theology to suggest that an angel could be the mediator between God and man. True, angels were used by God to inspire parts of the Bible and give the law (Gal. 3:19), but reconciliation and redemption required far more than any angel could give. An angel could not represent God to man or man to God. A mediator must be both; angels are neither. Also, angels are lower than God and higher than humans. But in truth, angels have far more in common with humans than with God (like us they are finite, not omniscient, etc.). No angel was ever God or human. There never has been a "God-angel" or "angel-man." If there were, he could serve as a mediator between angels and God or angels and men but not between God and humans.

To suggest that Jesus was an angel is to deny that He is the true Mediator or that He was truly a man. No mere man could serve as the perfect Mediator. Adam could not, even before the fall. Moses, Peter, or Mary could not either. Priests served as lesser mediators, and so did prophets. But we need a still higher priest and prophet to be the perfect Mediator. The book of Hebrews shows that Jesus Christ alone qualifies. He is God; He is superior to angels, prophets, and priests, and yet He is also sinless man. This God-man is uniquely qualified to be the Mediator.

JESUS IS

Both David's Son and David's Lord

The Jewish religious leaders tried to trap Jesus to have Him arrested, but they failed. Jesus turned the tables on them and asked them a question they could not answer: "What do you think about the Christ? Whose Son is He?" They replied correctly, "The Son of David" (Matt. 22:42; cf. 1:1; 20:31). The term *Son of David* was a special title for the Messiah (Christ). He was descended from David (Matt. 1). But the Jews were dumbfounded when Jesus then asked them, "If David then calls Him 'Lord,' how is He his Son?" (22:45). They couldn't answer.

The answer is obvious to those who know their Bibles. Jesus was physically descended from David through His mother, Mary. Joseph was not His biological father—God was His Father. In His deity, Jesus was Lord of David. In His humanity, He was Son of David. Thus, in His two natures, Jesus was David's son and Lord (cf. Rom. 1:3).

We can use this great truth when we read the Psalms. The Lord that David sang to and about was the Lord Jesus, as in, "The LORD [Jesus] is my shepherd" (Ps. 23:1; cf. John 10:11).

Those who deny Christ's divinity are as stumped as the Pharisees were. But ironically, David's son and Lord was right in front of the Pharisees then and is right before us spiritually as we read the New Testament today.

JESUS IS
to Be Loved as God

Jesus said that the greatest of all commandments is "You shall love the LORD your God with all your heart, with all your soul, and with all your mind" (Matt. 22:37). No commandment is greater than this (v. 38) for the simple reason that God is greater than all else. God deserves our greatest love and will not settle for second place. To love anything or anyone more than God is highly irreverent. It would make a love-idol of someone, as some do. God is as jealous for this love as He is for worship, for ultimate love and worship go together.

It is like marriage. A man may have a general love for all persons, but he reserves a special greater love for his wife (Eph. 5:25). We must love God both quantitatively more and qualitatively different than any other. The reason is that God is quantitatively greater and qualitatively different than all others.

Now Jesus also said, "He who loves father or mother more than Me is not worthy of Me. And he who loves son or daughter more than Me is not worthy of Me" (Matt. 10:37). Jesus demands that we love Him above all others, even our closest relatives and spouses. We must love Jesus above all people and in a qualitatively different way. That is because He is God. The second greatest commandment is to love our fellow men (Matt. 22:39). It is not enough to love Jesus like that. We must love Him as the God-man, and in a beautiful way, we thereby keep the two greatest commandments in the fullest sense.

Not to love the Lord Jesus Christ brings utter damnation (1 Cor. 16:22). That could never be said about any mere man or angel but only of God. Ephesians 6:24 has a greeting that implies a blessing for all who "love our Lord Jesus Christ in sincerity."

JESUS IS
the God–Man

There has never been a more important hyphen in history than the one in the term God-man. Jesus is fully God and fully man. When He became a man, He did not cease to be God. When He returned to heaven, He did not cease to be man. Theologians call this the hypostatic union—two natures in one person. It is somewhat like the Trinity—three persons with one nature. It is a deep, deep mystery (1 Tim. 3:16). No one has ever fully understood it. We bow in holy awe and amazement before Jesus the God-man.

Even in the time of the apostles, there were heretics who denied that Jesus was fully man. These Gnostics, especially those called Docetists, said that since matter is necessarily evil, Jesus did not take on a material body. John condemned this as anti-Christian (1 John 4:2–3; 2 John 1:7). This same John repeatedly stated that Jesus is fully God. To deny Christ's deity is as anti-Christian as to deny His humanity. He is both God and man, and what God has joined, let no man put asunder.

It will not do to say, "I can't understand how He could be both. He had to be either God or man but not both." That is the wrong approach. We must submit our minds to God and ask, "What saith the Scriptures?" Scripture teaches that Jesus is both God and man. Just because we cannot fully understand it is no reason why we should deny it, any more than we should deny the doctrine of the Trinity.

Jesus is the unique God-man. We cannot say, "God is God, and man is man, and never the twain shall meet." The twain meet in Jesus Christ. True, God-as-God is not a man (Num. 23:19) and man-as-man is not God or a god (Ezek. 28:2). Christ is the one and only God-man. The divine nature was not humanized nor the human nature deified. Jesus is not a man who became a god, as Mormons say, nor an angel who became a man, as Jehovah's Witnesses say. He is God become the God-man. Nor is He half-God and half-man but fully God and fully man. The heart of the gospel is that Jesus Christ is and always shall be the unique God-man.

There Is No Verse in the Bible
That Says Jesus Is Not God

Hundreds of verses in the Bible explicitly or implicitly say that Jesus Christ is God. Some stand on their own; others teach it when compared with other verses. We have looked at hundreds of such verses and have concentrated on the explicit ones.

Those who deny the deity of Christ sometimes say, "Show me a Bible verse that says 'Jesus is God' in those exact words, or I will not believe it." By that logic we could reply, "Show me a Bible verse that says 'Jesus is not God.'" There is no verse that explicitly or implicitly denies that Jesus is God. It may say that Jesus was a man (e.g., 1 Tim. 2:5), but it never says that Jesus was just a man. It never pronounces a curse on those who believe Jesus is God, though it condemns those who deny He was a man (1 John 4:3). Such statements are conspicuous by their absence in light of the many that explicitly teach His deity. This is overwhelmingly conclusive. If Jesus is not God, we should expect at least one verse to explicitly say so—but there is none. On the other hand, if He is God, we should expect to find at least one that explicitly says so—and there are many. To twist the many explicit verses and appeal to absent verses is to twist Scripture, which is condemned in 2 Peter 3:16.

The Bible frequently denies that certain persons were more than mere men. For example, Jesus is called the Light in John's gospel. John 1:8 says of John the Baptist, "He was not that Light, but was sent to bear witness of that Light." Similarly, when people wondered if John was the Messiah, "He confessed, and did not deny, but confessed, 'I am not the Christ'" (John 1:20). In Acts 14:11, the people of Lystra mistakenly thought that Paul and Barnabas were gods, which they explicitly denied in verse 15. But there is not a single verse anywhere in which Jesus denied being God, even in situations where people believed and said He was God (such as Thomas, John 20:28). If He was not God, why did He not simply and plainly say so? He often corrected the Jews' wrong ideas and the errors of His followers. But in this context, He rebuked them for not believing He was who He said He was—God (cf. John 8:25). "If it were not so, I would have told you" (John 14:2).

When Cornelius knelt before Peter in an act of worship, Peter rebuked him and said, "Stand up; I myself am also a man" (Acts 10:26). Why did not Christ rebuke those who knelt before Him in an act of worship? Because they did the right thing. Jesus never said anything like "I am only a man, not God."

Only one verse would be sufficient to prove Jesus is or is not God. The Bible's unanimous testimony is that Christ is God. It asserts His deity without a single dissenting vote. The Bible is God's word, so this is God Himself testifying that Jesus is God. We believe Jesus is God for one reason: because God says so.

Conclusion

No doubt there are still more proofs in the Bible than these one hundred. But the ones we've considered here are more than sufficient. The overwhelming testimony of Scripture is that Jesus Christ is indeed God.

This puts unbelievers in an uncomfortable position. They must either believe Jesus is God on the authority of the Bible or deny the Bible. Some choose the latter. They continue to deny the obvious and distort the Bible's clear teaching because of their presuppositions to the contrary. Fortunately, there are still others who decide to believe. If you are still an unbeliever, I encourage you to consider what God Himself has said. To disbelieve God is to call Him a liar (1 John 5:10). To believe God is the only reasonable thing to do. Believing in Jesus Christ as God opens the door to many wonderful blessings. May God grant you the privilege of seeing this great truth.

Recommended Reading

Armstrong, John H., ed. *The Glory of Christ*. Wheaton, Ill.: Crossway, 2002.

Bavinck, Herman. *Reformed Dogmatics*, 3:233–319. Grand Rapids: Baker Academic, 2003.

Berkhof, Louis. *Systematic Theology*, 305–30. Grand Rapids: Eerdmans, 1974.

Berkouwer, G. C. *The Person of Christ*. Grand Rapids: Eerdmans, 1954.

Boettner, Loraine. *Studies in Theology*, 140–269. Philadelphia: Presbyterian and Reformed, 1962.

Bowman, Robert M., Jr. *Jehovah's Witnesses, Jesus Christ, and the Gospel of John*. Grand Rapids: Baker, 1989.

Bowman, Robert M., Jr., and J. Ed. Komoszewski. *Putting Jesus in His Place: The Case for the Deity of Christ*. Grand Rapids: Kregel, 2007.

Brakel, Wilhelmus à. *The Christian's Reasonable Service*, 1:493–516. Ligonier, Pa.: Soli Deo Gloria, 1992.

Bright, Bill. *Discover the Real Jesus*. Wheaton, Ill.: Tyndale House, 2004.

Brown, Charles. *The Divine Glory of Christ*. Edinburgh: Banner of Truth, 1982.

Calvin, John. *Institutes of the Christian Religion*, 1.2.12–14 (1:464–93). Philadelphia: Westminster Press, 1960.

Capes, David B. *The Divine Christ*. Grand Rapids: Baker, 2018.

Chafer, Lewis Sperry. *Systematic Theology*, 1:318–96. Dallas: Dallas Seminary Press, 1975.

Dabney, Robert Lewis. *Systematic Theology*, 183–93. Edinburgh: Banner of Truth, 1985.

Edwards, Jonathan. *The Works of Jonathan Edwards*, 2:499–510. Edinburgh: Banner of Truth, 1974.

Erickson, Millard J. *Christian Theology*, 2:683–704. Grand Rapids: Baker, 1984.

———. *The Word Became Flesh*. Grand Rapids: Baker, 1991.

Ferguson, Sinclair B., and Derek W. H. Thomas. *Ichthus: Jesus Christ, God's Son, the Saviour*. Edinburgh: Banner of Truth, 2017.

Frame, John. *The Doctrine of God*, 647–85. Phillipsburg, N.J.: P&R, 2002.

———. *Systematic Theology*, 877–98. Phillipsburg, N.J.: P&R, 2013.

Geisler, Norman. *Systematic Theology*, 2:597–631. Minneapolis: Bethany House, 2003.

Gerhard, Johann. *On Christ*. St. Louis: Concordia Publishing House, 2009.

Gerstner, John H. *A Primer on the Deity of Christ*. Phillipsburg, N.J.: Presbyterian and Reformed, 1984.

Grudem, Wayne. *Systematic Theology*, 529–67. Grand Rapids: Zondervan, 1994.

Gurbikian, Gregory. *The Deity of Christ in the Old & New Testaments*. Maitland, Fla.: Xulon Press, 2011.

Harris, Murray J. *Jesus as God*. Grand Rapids: Baker, 1992.

———. *Three Crucial Questions about Jesus*. Grand Rapids: Baker, 1994.

Heppe, Heinrich. *Reformed Dogmatics*, 410–47. Grand Rapids: Baker, 1978.

Hodge, Charles. *Systematic Theology*, 1:482–521. Grand Rapids: Eerdmans, 1982.

Horton, Michael. *The Christian Faith*, 446–82. Grand Rapids: Zondervan, 2011.

Hyde, Daniel R. *God with Us: Knowing the Mystery of Who Jesus Is*. Grand Rapids: Reformation Heritage Books, 2007.

Jeffrey, Douglas K. *Logikos: A Comprehensive Reference to Biblical Evidence of the Trinity and the Deity of Christ*. Bloomington, Ind.: WestBow, 2019.

LaHaye, Tim. *Jesus: Who Is He?* Sisters, Ore.: Multnomah, 1996.

Lanier, Greg. *Is Jesus God?* Wheaton, Ill.: Crossway, 2020.

Liddon, H. P. *The Divinity of Our Lord and Saviour Jesus Christ*. 1897. Reprint, Minneapolis: Klock & Klock, 1978.

Limbaugh, David. *The True Jesus*. Washington, D.C.: Regnery, 2017.

MacArthur, John. *The Deity of Christ*. Chicago: Moody, 2017.

MacArthur, John, ed. *High King of Heaven*. Chicago: Moody, 2018.

MacArthur, John, and Richard Mayhue, eds. *Biblical Doctrine: A Systematic Summary of Bible Truth*, 202–4, 255–58, 273–74. Wheaton, Ill.: Crossway, 2017.

Machen, J. Gresham. *The Person of Jesus*. Philadelphia: Westminster Seminary Press, 2017.

McDowell, Josh. *More Than a Carpenter*. Wheaton, Ill.: Tyndale House, 1977.

McDowell, Josh, and Bart Larson. *Jesus: A Biblical Defense of His Deity*. San Bernardino: Here's Life Publishers, 1983.

Morgan, Christopher W., and Robert A. Peterson, eds. *The Deity of Christ*. Wheaton, Ill.: Crossway, 2011.

Muller, Richard A. *Post-Reformation Reformed Dogmatics*, 4:275–332. Grand Rapids: Baker Academic, 2003.

Oden, Thomas. *The Word of Life*. San Francisco: Harper & Row, 1989.

Owen, John. *The Works of John Owen*. Vol. 1. Edinburgh: Banner of Truth, 1965.

Reymond, Robert L. *Jesus, Divine Messiah*. Phillipsburg, N.J.: Presbyterian and Reformed, 1990.

———. *A New Systematic Theology of the Christian Faith*, 214–312. Nashville: Thomas Nelson, 1998.

Sanferrare, Charles J. *50 Reasons Jesus Christ Is God*. No city: Self-published, 2016.

Shedd, William G. T. *Dogmatic Theology*, 3rd ed., 257–71. Phillipsburg, N.J.: P&R, 2003.

Strobel, Lee. *The Case for Christ*. Grand Rapids: Zondervan, 1998.

Strong, Augustus Hopkins. *Systematic Theology*, 681–700. Old Tappan, N.J.: Fleming H. Revell, 1974.

Turretin, Francis. *Institutes of Elenctic Theology*, 1:282–302. Phillipsburg, N.J.: P&R, 1992.

Vos, Geerhardus. *Reformed Dogmatics*. Vol. 3. Bellingham, Wa.: Lexham Press, 2014.

Walvoord, John F. *Jesus Christ Our Lord*. Chicago: Moody Press, 1969.

Warfield, Benjamin B. *Biblical and Theological Studies*, 22–126. Phillipsburg, N.J.: Presbyterian and Reformed, 1968.

———. *The Lord of Glory*. 1907. Reprint, Grand Rapids: Zondervan, n.d.

———. *The Person and Work of Christ*. Philadelphia: Presbyterian and Reformed, 1970.

Wellum, Stephen J. *God the Son Incarnate*. Wheaton, Ill.: Crossway, 2015.

Zodhiates, Spiros. *Was Christ God?* Grand Rapids: Eerdmans, 1966.

TRUTH FOR LIFE®

THE BIBLE-TEACHING MINISTRY OF **ALISTAIR BEGG**

The mission of Truth For Life is to teach the Bible with clarity and relevance so that unbelievers will be converted, believers will be established, and local churches will be strengthened.

Daily Program
Each day, Truth For Life distributes the Bible teaching of Alistair Begg across the U.S. and in several locations outside of the U.S. through 2,000 radio outlets. To find a radio station near you, visit **truthforlife.org/stationfinder**.

Free Teaching
The daily program, and Truth For Life's entire teaching library of over 3,000 Bible-teaching messages, can be accessed for free online at **truthforlife.org** and through Truth For Life's mobile app, which can be download for free from your app store.

At-Cost Resources
Books and audio studies from Alistair Begg are available for purchase at cost, with no markup. Visit **truthforlife.org/store**.

Where to Begin?
If you're new to Truth For Life and would like to know where to begin listening and learning, find starting point suggestions at **truthforlife.org/firststep**. For a full list of ways to connect with Truth For Life, visit **truthforlife.org/subscribe**.

Contact Truth For Life
P.O. Box 398000 Cleveland, Ohio 44139
phone 1 (888) 588-7884   **email** letters@truthforlife.org **truthforlife.org**